RADICAL
INTEGRITY

RADICAL INTEGRITY

21 Ways to Heal Your Inner Child and Create a True Adult

KATHLEEN BROOKS, Ph.D.

ethicalife

Ethicalife Press | San Diego | California

Copyright © 2012 Ethicalife Press

ISBN 978-0-9840272-0-0 paperback
      978-0-9840272-1-7 eBook

Published by Ethicalife Press
San Diego, CA
858-836-1153
www.ethicalife.com

Publishing Consulting and Product Development:
BookStudio, LLC, www.bookstudiobooks.com
Book Design:
Bill Greaves, Concept West, www.billgreaves.com
Author Photo:
Kat Miner

Printed in the United States of America

To my beloved children: Tracy, Jamie, and David

To my grandchildren: Kye, Elisa, Sage, Sabrina, Calleagh, Ethan, and David

*To the father of my children: Bob, whose commitment
to healing I respect and honor*

*To all the children of the world, young and old, who deserve
to live in a safe and sane world*

Table of Contents

Introduction

Like many of us, I have struggled with adulthood. In fact, I didn't want to become an adult; my parents made adulthood look decidedly dull, difficult, and uninspiring! Yet, in doing that, they provided the inspiration for this book. Their struggles instilled in me a deep longing to seek a better, more fulfilling way to live my life. This book represents a compilation of the philosophies that have guided and inspired me throughout life to become what I call a True Adult.

My first guide was Buckminster Fuller, one of the greatest minds of the twentieth century, who believed that integrity would save the planet. My inspiration was *The I Ching,* the ancient Chinese Book of Changes, originally compiled to assist the ruling dynasties in China. A teacher in graduate school introduced me to this ancient text and I have come to see it as a kind of Holy Grail for humanity, with its wise guidance on all the topics that humans have to deal with. Wisdom is the antidote to ignorance, and I have tried to present these timeless principles in a way that makes them useful today.

This ancient text emphasizes how the family is the source of our humanity. It was a profound moment when I understood that we all have to *learn* how to be human from other humans in that basic unit we call the family. This simple awareness revealed how humanity perpetuates the beliefs and behaviors we all share. The main source of our suffering is the perception that we are powerless, which we feel when we lack self-esteem. This sense of powerlessness and lack of self-esteem prevents us from becoming truly mature and capable of handling life in a competent and fulfilling way.

We learn self-esteem in our families. If our families fail to instill self-esteem, we suffer. But by learning how to become what

I call a True Adult, one who *chooses* what beliefs and behaviors to adopt rather than living from learned and unquestioned beliefs and behaviors, we can *develop* the character that creates self-esteem and makes healthy, life-enhancing choices, no matter what our families taught us. We will change over the years; that is inevitable. As a True Adult, we can grow into our full potential as powerful human beings.

Each of the *21 Ways* presented in the second part of this book assists this process. They promote the integrity that guides us in living lives that are empowered by choices that create self-esteem. If you are one of the many people who have suffered abuse, neglect, depression, addiction, and the other plagues that have haunted the human race, these principles are imperative for your healing. They are radical principles, because they involve the engagement of personal choice, personal truth, and personal integrity, qualities that require a willingness to question the status quo and act from personal conviction rather than going along with the crowd. They are as powerful today as they were centuries ago because they promote and sustain the personal power and dignity that living with radical integrity can bring.

This book explores the importance of creating and maintaining a successful relationship with yourself and others through adhering to values that impart the dignity and compassion that integrity brings to every area of life. It challenges false assumptions that we have inherited from our culture about ways to think and behave that are disempowering and damaging, while honoring the proven principle that the quality of your relationships is what ultimately determines the success of all your endeavors, both personal and professional. That quality depends upon the degree of personal power that you can access to offset the victim consciousness that has plagued mankind for centuries. Embracing your personal power is the only way to create the self-esteem necessary for having fulfilling relationships.

The *21 Ways* offer invaluable assistance in healing your Inner Child and achieving the personal power that supports a True Adult. You will feel genuinely good about yourself when using these as guidelines for how to think and act. They can be read in order or, if you prefer, you can pick one that interests you and start there. Try to consciously practice each *Way* for at least a month or so to make it a habit. Work these principles into your daily life until they require little effort, becoming part of your being.

May you be inspired to use these *21 Ways* to nurture the radical integrity vital to healing our lives and our planet. Together, may we change the world for the better, creating a safer and saner world for us and for the children who are watching us.

Feel free to contact me with comments or questions.

Kathleen Brooks, Ph.D.
San Diego, CA

PART I

Hope for the Future: Creating True Adults and Empowering Children with Radical Integrity

"The family is society in embryo; it is the native soil on which performance of moral duty is made easy through natural affection, so that within a small circle a basis of moral practice is created, and this is later widened to include human relationships in general. When the family is in order, all the social relationships of mankind will be in order."

—*The I Ching*, Hexagram #37, The Family

We are formed by our families. Nothing is more important to understanding what it means to be human than this.

Although the way our families operate has worked for the survival of the species, it has kept us surviving rather than thriving as a species. We emerge battered and bruised, broken and bewildered. We are all miracles, waiting to be birthed within the family. Too many of us die, however, never having experienced the birth of our full potential!

It's time for us to admit that it's hard to become a healthy, happy adult. It's a long journey that must be guided by healthy, happy parents. You are lucky indeed if you had such parents. Too many do not. Others assume they had a wonderful childhood only to find themselves floundering as grown-ups. Too many of us become permanent victims of a life we don't feel equipped to handle and scared to death that people will find out we're faking it (that is, if we even *know* that we're faking it). Too many of us are looking for someone else to provide the answers and then we end up becoming the pawns of anyone who seems to have the answers. Too many of us are frightened and insecure and lost. Too many of us don't know who we are and are therefore living a life divorced from our own truth.

Here's a typical scenario: You've gone to the best school you could get into; you live in the best neighborhood you can; you use the right slang; you marry the right person (even if you had to leave a few partners that weren't right); you shop at the right stores and wear the right clothes; you really work hard at being accepted and liked and you really do want to fit in. But there's a catch: These things are not making you feel fulfilled or empowered. Despite all you have, you haven't fulfilled your dreams. All that potential got drowned in concerns about pursuing things that didn't really fulfill you and people who didn't meet your expectations or support your values. On top of that, you have a lot of debt and responsibility that feels heavy instead of empowering. Maybe your kids didn't turn out the way you had envisioned. They may fail in school, they may do drugs, they may have an unwanted pregnancy or an eating disorder. Your marriage is empty and your career never took off. What happened?!

You may know it; or you may not, but somewhere along the way you lost touch with who you really are.

Here's another typical scenario: You've refused to live the conventional life. You dropped out of school; you don't care how you look and/or you enjoy the disdain of people who notice your tattoos; you refuse to play the game and revel in being a rebel; you either refuse to have kids or you let your kids fend for themselves. You work hard at being different and are proud of not fitting in with those middle-class drones. You refuse to care what the neighbors think of your untrimmed lawn and the old cars parked in your driveway. You are amazed when your kids choose to live in the suburbs and work hard to have all the things you thought they could do without. What happened?!

You may know it; or you may not, but somewhere along the way you lost touch with who you really are.

You may not exactly relate to these scenarios, but each of us is creating our own scenarios, either from what we really are or from what we think we ought to be. Chances are that the people who are in one scenario judge the ones who are in another. We learn to judge what is different, what is uncomfortable. We live in an "us" versus "them" world that extends out to include other cultures and countries. We learn to fear "them," and there is enormous pressure to adopt the characteristics displayed by other people we identify as "us."

During the twentieth century, the changes in the world increased at an alarming rate. It hasn't slowed down a bit as we've moved into the twenty-first. All the old labels are being stretched and questioned. Instant access to events around the globe creates a new awareness that includes an expanded but also questionable notion of just who are "us" and "them."

Discoveries of the new physics have challenged our fundamental perceptions of reality, and these discoveries are becoming a part of people's awareness everywhere. Changes in our ways of perceiving and thinking are being achieved by ever-new technologies that keep us all instantly linked. The old ways are rapidly being replaced, creating a more inclusive way to be human beings. What that means for you as an individual is that there is a freedom to question the scenario that you inherited from your family and create one that takes into account your fundamental nature, your personality and your passions, as well as providing a deep sense of personal fulfillment. We are all involved in a time of discovering what we love and what works for us, who we are and who we want to be. We are indeed doing what Buckminster Fuller urged: discovering integrity.

Discovering Integrity

Integrity: "State or quality of being complete, undivided or unbroken; unimpaired state, soundness, purity; moral soundness, honesty, uprightness."
—Webster's New Collegiate Dictionary

Integrity is honoring your personal uniqueness while at the same time acknowledging the uniqueness of others. It is honoring that we are all humans, but each of us is on a unique path. It is honoring that there is room for each of us to be different and that each of our differences is a gift to the other. Doing what everyone else does in order to be accepted is not integrity; neither is rebelling against what everyone is doing just to be different. Integrity is acting from a deep inner knowing of who *you* are, what *you* feel and what *you* want. Integrity comes from a place of congruence with who you are and what you do; it requires knowing yourself and being honest with yourself and others about it, then acting on this knowledge.

I first encountered the term "integrity" when I was a young mother in my twenties. One rainy day, sitting in my living room while the kids napped, I read an article in *LIFE* magazine about a great visionary and humanitarian and scientist and … well, he was pretty accomplished. His name was Buckminster Fuller and he was not only the inventor of the geodesic dome, among many things, but a philosopher who considered integrity the single most important quality to which people should aspire. Indeed, he saw it as the answer to the problems of the modern world.

I had never even thought about integrity, but instinctively I knew it was important and that I wanted to learn more about it.

I was beginning to suspect that I was far too preoccupied with doing the "right" thing (which actually meant doing what everybody else expected) to really have the integrity that came from knowing who I was and what I wanted.

It was the sixties, those infamous years of sex, drugs, and rock 'n roll; long hair was standard, for both boys and girls. I graduated from college in 1961 and my mother insisted I cut my long hair to walk down the aisle at my wedding. Ever the dutiful child, I complied and then cried myself to sleep (integrity was unavailable to me at the time because I hadn't matured enough). Other, braver kids were challenging the rigid, materialistic, rather shallow behavior that was the norm for the fifties. The hippie movement had started a revolution that some believed would be the demise of our nation; others saw it as our salvation. Those were radical times. While the original meaning of radical is "fundamental, vital, original," the term expanded during the sixties to mean "beyond the pale or the norm, stretching the limits of what's acceptable." The "radical" of the sixties connoted things that were out of the ordinary, daring, unorthodox, maybe even a little scary or crazy.

The way the term "integrity" hit me, a few years into my marriage at the young age of twenty-one on that rainy day as my kids napped, was not only radical in the traditional meaning (fundamental and vital), but also unorthodox and daring. Bucky (as Buckminster was affectionately known) was right! Once I started paying attention, I realized that integrity had become all too rare in the twentieth century. That day I put "radical" with "integrity" and the name for this book, Radical Integrity, was born.

Now, at the beginning of the twenty-first century, several marriages, several degrees, and many experiences later, including the development of a keen awareness of the lies, withheld truths, and broken agreements that have become the norm for many of us, I have finally learned enough and lived enough to speak about it.

While some incredible events have occurred that have made life truly wonderful, life has also become more and more stressful since the sixties. We have always lived in a world where we have to worry about whom we can trust. (Even the cavemen fought for territory and food.) Today that stress has taken on global proportions, with a long war in the Middle East, a global recession, and atomic radiation placing all of us in imminent threat. One of the main reasons life has become much harder is because humans don't do well when they don't feel safe, and it can be downright scary and painful when you look out at the world today. You may be having trouble maintaining trust in our governments, in our institutions, and in others. Without trust, humans don't feel safe; you may be going to a lot of trouble and using a lot of energy just trying to protect yourself. And when you're protecting yourself, you shut down to learning. It's just how the brain works.

Safety is the foundation of trust, a fundamental need, and the cornerstone of integrity.

We are in this together and I need you to be safe in order to prosper; you need me in the same way. And because we need each other, I am optimistic. Integrity, while not necessarily in vogue, has not died. I can tell, because one thing I've noticed over the years is that a sure way to make people angry and defensive is to tell them they have no integrity. Most of us don't want to be accused of lacking integrity, even if we aren't sure what it is! But integrity is too important to be relegated to some popular buzzword bantered around by people who lack it! In a world where so many of us feel broken, incomplete, and impaired, where honesty is hard to come by and morality is up for grabs, it's time to bring integrity to the forefront of our attention. It's the healing force that our troubled times call for! And it has to start with you and me.

We're talking about integrity when we say, "Walk your talk." It has also been described as being congruent in word and deed. You experience integrity when someone is trustworthy, when someone matches up, when what people say is what they do. Integrity is also present when you do the right thing, not the easy thing, when you're consistently honest but can also apologize for your slipups (because we're all imperfect humans) instead of blaming others. When someone's intentions are pure, and not motivated by hidden agendas, greed, or lust, you are in the presence of someone who has integrity. You can relax around people who have it because you know they're not out to hurt you or use you. You can count on them and they can count on you. Everyone can relax!

There is an important individual component of integrity that I would like to add. That is the power and the congruence that comes from acknowledging and honoring your multidimensional nature. Each of us is a complex unit of many parts. We are not only physical beings; we are mental, emotional, perceptual, and spiritual beings. We have integrity when we are congruent in all our parts, when what we say is consistent with how we feel, how we act, and what we think. As Gay Hendricks says in *The Big Leap,* it really has to do with "wholeness and completeness."

Nurturing Integrity

"To a child, abandonment is death. The two most basic needs of a child are to know my parents are okay and that I matter. Give your Inner Child permission, protection and potency to think, feel, want and do in relationship to self, other and world."
—John Bradshaw

Integrity is inherent in your nature, but it must be nurtured by people who model it for you as you move through the developmental years of childhood. That modeling needs to be multidimensional.

Those who teach you can't preach it and not do it, although many people try, as we have witnessed throughout history. I guess that's what makes nurturing integrity a challenge. You can't buy it, like a new car or a new lipstick, and you absolutely can't fake it. If integrity is to be learned, it must be imparted, i.e., modeled by parents who lovingly take on the task of nurturing their children by example. These nurturing parents are willing to know and accept who and what their children uniquely are and trust that uniqueness. It always requires a deep commitment to honesty. It also demands facing the truth that our children are mirrors that show us the truth, good and bad. For anyone, looking in the mirror can be daunting, and nothing is more revealing than the mirrors our children provide. That's why people have been blaming children for so long. It seems easier than admitting the truth they are looking at!

Parents too often need their children to shore up their own flagging, damaged self-esteem. You are born with an innate ability to make sense of your own reality, but parents are required to catalyze those instincts. If your personality, your natural way of being, your authentic expression of self is recognized, supported, and encouraged by your parents, it becomes easy and natural to be *who you really are*. This is integrity. But if your parents need you to be the way *they* want, if they are uncomfortable with anything that doesn't fit their idea of "right" or anything that makes them look "bad," then your natural integrity is severely hindered. Your original impulse as a young child to tell the truth quickly adapts to figuring a way to get parental attention and approval. Being the smart creature you are, you quickly learn how effectively a little lie works to keep you out of trouble and make your parents happy. It's so easy to do and seems so harmless. (I ask people in my workshops when they first remember lying, and the average age is about three, the age at which most of us can really talk.)

Often the truth requires doing the hard thing, the uncomfortable thing, and we humans often resist that, especially when we expect some kind of punishment in response. By the time children reach adolescence, where image is everything, lying has too often been perfected to an art form! By adulthood, unless you're still childishly naïve, you don't even expect others to tell you the whole truth. You've learned to be a little wary or even downright cynical. Some people never develop a conscience and become pathological liars, which every mental health professional knows is hard to cure.

My Personal Journey

"Lessons repeat themselves until we learn them."
—Dan Millman

My own childhood was an interesting study in the power of lies and secrets to destroy (in other words, it was marked by the destruction that a lack of parental integrity can create). My first suspicion that there was much I didn't know and also much that had been kept from me started in grade school. My mother was more interested in housecleaning than in me. I pushed this out of my awareness as much as possible because it made me very sad and uncomfortable, but visits to other homes revealed just how unavailable my mother was. My father was distinctly uncomfortable around children and preoccupied with work and reading his books about the Civil War. I wondered why and worried that he mostly ignored me because I was a bad girl.

As I got older, I had the distinct feeling that I couldn't really trust my parents. They weren't real to me. My sister and I had many talks about how we didn't really understand why our parents were married, but we were distracted by our own lives and too busy with our own concerns to see how that would impact us later. And in other ways I was very aware that I had it much better than many of the kids in my neighborhood. There was a lot of poverty in the small town where we lived, so my life looked pretty good on the outside. After all, I had been on trips to big cities and faraway places while many of my friends had never even left the small, rural county we lived in.

Full realization of my issues with trust and love came in my twenties, when I was in the throes of my first marriage. I was a young mother, fresh out of college and tending to my beautiful baby girl. I realized that although I had a college degree, there was so much I didn't know. (It even occurred to me that maybe this was the main purpose of education—to make you aware of how little you know!) Some parts of life, like this tiny child in my arms, were just too mysterious to rationally comprehend. What did I want to pass on to my child? The only thing I was sure of was that much that had been passed on to me felt scary, unpalatable, and destructive. I hadn't really wanted to be an adult because my parents made adulthood look hard and boring. I didn't know how to relate to babies even though I had read a bunch of books. I didn't understand it then, and it's taken a very long time for it to become clear, but the truth is I wasn't properly attached to my parents, which made it difficult for me to be a parent myself. Parenting with integrity had not been modeled for me. Instead, as a child I was insecure and always worried that I would do something wrong and incur my mother's wrath or more of my father's withdrawal.

What I did know is that while I had been blessed with a lot of talents and brains, a good education, and a lovely home, I was unsure and often afraid. My parents had not understood that I needed their "permission, protection and potency," as John Bradshaw, author of *Healing the Shame That Binds You* and a pioneer in dealing with dysfunctional families, revealed to me only after I finished my degree in psychology many years later. Meanwhile, I felt this deep insecurity, and furthermore, I felt ashamed of it. I hid all of this very well, because I was smart and had a big personality, plus I was used to performing, having done so for my parents' dinner parties since I was a young girl. I played the piano and sang harmonies to my sister's melodies. Early on, I figured out that a little charm went a long way toward winning over people. The rest was my secret.

Despite the accolades and awards of school, my insecurity simmered below the surface and affected me in many ways. I remained secretly afraid that I just wasn't good enough and actually was undeserving of the attention I received. I was the salutatorian of my graduating class, but agonized that nobody seemed interested in knowing the real me. After all, I was more than a walking brain. I had matured physically without knowing who I was or what I wanted. I was too busy figuring out what everybody else needed, trying hard to make my mother and father happy, and terrified at how unsuccessful I was at doing that. I had learned to be afraid of upsetting people, so I went along with others just to keep the peace.

That's the essence of what I learned to do as a child—make others happy. I was taught that anything else was selfish. While I had done well in school, I was plagued by a feeling of failure because, as hard as I tried, I just never really succeeded in my quest of making my parents happy. The approval I sought from my parents seldom materialized, and criticism was all too familiar. I remember, as a grown-up, asking my mother why she never acknowledged me; she told me that she was afraid I would get conceited. I assured her that she had succeeded because I didn't have an ounce of conceit in my body. I was still having problems believing in myself even though I had completed my doctorate degree!

So here I was, a young mother, full of unmet needs, lots of questions, and seething with insecurities. I had married my high school sweetheart the week after I graduated from college, despite the fact that I didn't really like or trust him; I pitied him and we certainly weren't friends. We seemed locked in a strange sexual dance that both horrified me and intrigued me. He was good-looking and I knew we would make beautiful babies, but the truth was I had no idea what love was. I knew I needed it but I didn't really know what it looked like. I remember as a child asking my mother if she loved Daddy, and her terse reply was, "Of course I do." I thought to myself, "If that's love, I don't want any part of it." So I settled for the quick fix of a marriage, just like all my sorority sisters were doing, hoping that would somehow heal my insecurities and reveal the mysteries of love to me.

In my heart, I knew I had married for the wrong reasons. But I was terrified of being on my own; I was not equipped emotionally to handle a career. The world seemed confusing and scary, and I didn't have any idea how to support myself and become independent. My parents had shielded me from many things, even death (I wasn't allowed to attend funerals, even my grandfather's), but I was emotionally inhibited and still terribly dependent on others' opinions and approval. Although many things in our small town intrigued me, they were hidden from me and it scared me too much to explore. My foray into the big, wide world of college had been fun, but I quickly reverted after graduation into what I was familiar with because that was what my mother had modeled. I retreated from the bigger world, got married, and buried myself in the familiar roles of housewife and mother.

Three marriages and three divorces later (and a bunch of other lovers I never married), I'm happy to say I have learned much about love and relationships. Or as Marie Curie expressed in a much better way, "Nothing in life is to be feared. It is only to be understood." My willingness to understand why I did the things I did has served me well.

I now know that we learn how to relate to others primarily from our relationship with our parents and from watching their relationship with each other. So I had started off with a big handicap, because as much as my parents pretended otherwise, I knew they were not happy, with each other or with the lives they had been thrust into by virtue of me. They had to get married (they called them "shotgun weddings" back then) because my mother got pregnant with me shortly after she met my father, who had just finished law school and moved into the area where my mother was raised and was now teaching. I'm sure he seemed like a good catch to my mother and, in a small town, the only choice was to avoid scandal and get married. They look so uncomfortable in their wedding pictures; they really were strangers from two different worlds: my father with his ever-present cigarette and my mother somber and unsmiling.

My mother was a farmer's daughter; my father was from a wealthy Pittsburgh family. My father had really wanted to be a violinist, but it was out of the question in the family he came from. (The only choices that were acceptable were doctor or lawyer.) My mother had started to pursue an education in music (she had a lovely soprano voice), but the Great Depression had ended that dream so she returned to the small town where she had grown up, got certified, and became a teacher. Music was the only thing my parents had in common, but it turned out that it wasn't enough to make a good marriage. Before I started school, my mother was suffering from high blood pressure and depression and my father came home injured from World War II, struggled with alcoholism, and molested me. I put up with my father's advances because I felt special that he gave me that attention, plus it was the only touching I got from anyone except when I was sick. My parents were resentful and alienated from each other, two polite strangers playing at marriage as if it was their duty, but not enjoying it at all. This was the model I inherited and this was the model I perpetuated.

I believe I chose my family to learn the things I needed to evolve as a human being. From a very early age, I wanted to understand why two intelligent, talented, and basically good people couldn't manage to love each other and be happy. I was obsessed with love and wanted to understand why two people with so much going for them couldn't manage to give me the attention, approval, and love I knew I longed for. Although everything looked good on the surface, it never felt good; there was constant tension in our home. I often felt scared and angry. I was obsessed with understanding this, and that search has given great meaning to my life.

If my parents had known about integrity, I wonder if their lives would have been different. Maybe they would have both been happy if their lives were more fulfilling. With more awareness about integrity, perhaps my father would have been true to himself and pursued a career as a violinist, and found a way to express his sensitive heart through his music. With integrity as her guide, perhaps my mother would have found a way to continue her career as a singer and learned to express her passion through her music. All I knew was that their unhappiness tortured me. I almost felt guilty about wanting a better life because I had been blessed in many ways, but the thought of ending up like them seemed like a death sentence.

I finally realized that living a life devoted to the duty that was the only thing that kept my parents together wasn't making me happy. I hungrily explored this thing called integrity and searched for what gave my life meaning. Today I have no regrets; my parents' pain and suffering have taught me about love, compassion, and forgiveness. My own confusion about who I am gave me the impetus to find out what self-esteem is and how to cultivate it.

Learning from the Past

"You never change things by fighting the existing reality. To change something, build a new model that makes the existing model obsolete.
—R. Buckminster Fuller

My fascination with integrity opened a Pandora's box; I knew I needed to go much deeper in my exploration. I was thrilled when my search led me to my next discovery. A young professor from the graduate school I was attending turned me on to a fascinating ancient Chinese *Book of Changes, The I Ching.* A brilliant young man who had finished his doctorate by the age of twenty-one, he stopped me after class one day and told me he had a feeling that I would be interested in this book. It offered objective advice by answering your question with a reading, which you obtained by throwing three coins. That professor must have been very intuitive, because I sure was in need of advice! I had just separated from my first husband, finally admitting that I had married simply because I was afraid I couldn't make it on my own. My family was scandalized and I was scared to death. Here I was, going back to school so I could earn a living to support my three children on top of trying to raise them and take care of my home, with no idea of how to do this. (Day care was very uncommon back then.) All I knew was that I had to change and move on.

The I Ching did not disappoint me. More than anything I've ever read, it provided the guidance that I desperately needed. This wisdom has survived centuries of use by some of the most learned men in the world, from Confucius to Carl Jung. I worked with the hexagrams until I felt comfortable with their sometimes hidden meanings. I began to see the possibility of accepting myself and enjoying my humanity, rather than judging, worrying, and feeling sorry for myself. I also began to see the importance that family played in the development of humans.

To be human is to be gifted. By that, I mean that you are blessed with a profound number of gifts just by virtue of

being human. Some of them run in your family and some of them are uniquely yours.

You are at the top of nature's hierarchy, carrying within you both the instincts of reptiles and mammals and the unique human brains and body that allow you to function above and beyond anything else in the natural world. However, many of us have a hard time figuring out how to be human, how to utilize our unique capabilities so that we can enjoy life and all that it offers. Human history is filled with stories of suffering, pain, and fear. We humans have had to learn how to survive, how to create shelter and safety from the elements, how to feed and clothe ourselves, how to deal with sickness, childbirth, and a wide variety of physical and mental infirmities. We have persevered and thrived, through war and pestilence, to create magnificent mechanical and electrical inventions that make life very different from that of those who came before us.

But one thing has not changed throughout history, and that is our ability to coexist in peace with our fellow man. We've had to compete with each other to survive for so long that we haven't come to grips with how to cooperate so that all humans can share the benefits of the resources that our brilliant minds have created. Instead, we have a modern world where people are more disconnected and cynical than ever. Many don't know whom to trust and believe they have to compete for scarce resources.

This distrust of each other has created a moral/ethical dilemma in our modern world. The distrust starts in the family. Whether you see the world as a safe place or as a dangerous place starts in the family. Your relationship with your parents sets the tone for all your subsequent relationships. Seeing the universe as essentially benevolent starts with our parents' benevolence, their love of us, their attachment to us. Seeing the world as dangerous and threatening starts there, too. As Albert Einstein said, "The most important decision you will ever make is whether the universe is friendly or not." Unfortunately, most children don't realize this until the damage has already been done.

We learn about the world in our families. This is where the seeds of our potential are nurtured and tended. It's not in the schools or the church; it's in the home. If your home failed to nurture and tend the seeds, schools and churches cannot substitute for that loss. In fact, they reflect the same flaws that you see in your family. You must go to the source if you want to change. That source for all of us is the family.

Integrity and Ethics

Ethics: "The science of moral duty; the science of ideal human behavior."
—Webster's New Collegiate Dictionary

Ethics is the wellspring of integrity. If you don't examine your own personal values, and live a life that you are truly proud of, you are out of integrity and unethical.

For years, ethics has been the province of a few intellectuals, relegated to catching dust in the back corners of the library. My ethics class as an undergraduate was the most boring class I ever took. It seemed so heady, so irrelevant. It wasn't presented in a way that my heart could relate to, and the head without the heart can be a dangerous place.

What you must do is bring ethics out of the libraries and into your home by making it a living, breathing part of your everyday life! It is *unethical* humans, lacking moral values, personal power, and integrity, who are destroying not only our families and the social fabric, but also the democratic principles and even the environment that support our lives. It is unethical humans that create the unfriendly world that Einstein spoke about. It doesn't get more relevant than that!

There are three ethical dilemmas we face as we start the twenty-first century:

1. How to create peace, harmony, and goodwill on this planet by imparting a sense of personal empowerment within every human being.

2. How to empower the humans on this planet so they no longer experience themselves as victims of those in power, waiting for somebody else to find a solution to their suffering, but instead experience themselves as responsible and valued members of the human family.

3. How to create truly empowered, mature adults who are capable of and willing to act with integrity, that is, in ethical ways to end their suffering and do their part to restore peace and harmony on this planet.

Ancient prophecies predict that cataclysmic events are coming in our lifetime. If you pay attention to the media, it looks as though the doomsday forecasts may be accurate. Eruptions from Mother Earth in the form of hurricanes, floods, tsunamis, and earthquakes have created worldwide crises. Moral decay, social decay, and institutional and corporate decay are rampant. The battle between good and evil has certainly reached a fever pitch since the start of the new millennium. People in the Middle East are overthrowing their governments and looking to us for assistance. To add insult to injury, as a nation we are still grieving the loss of the Twin Towers, symbols of our might and power. This has been accompanied by shocking scandals involving people who have positions of power and authority among us. From presidents to CEOs, a dismaying lack of integrity has been uncovered and exposed, leaving many of us shaken, cynical, and despairing. As you watch prominent and esteemed people exposed on national television and dragged off in handcuffs, the clear distinction between the good guys and the bad guys has grown blurry. Trust in political and corporate leaders has been eroded. This lack of ethical leadership has created a great malaise among all of us that makes threats from abroad even more debilitating and doomsday forecasts more believable.

The blatant dishonesty and lack of ethics shown by leaders in this nation are creating havoc in our corporations, our churches, our government, and our schools. Only a willingness on the part of leaders to do the right thing, the moral thing, the virtuous thing can create the climate of stability and security so necessary for people and their endeavors. When leaders have this kind of integrity, their organizations prosper and people live with a sense of trust in their world. A culture lacking ethical, moral fiber soon fills in with fear the gaps that integrity and ethics have vacated. Nothing causes decay like fear! When the elite in our nation, those entrusted with great power and authority, are unethical, those of us who rely on these people for leadership and guidance have reason to quake.

Conscientious people are concerned about the climate of moral decay but many are at a loss for solutions that truly work. Often the solutions that have been tried were mere Band-Aids on a deep cancer. I've watched our education system flounder for years with programs that come and go while the problems remain and even worsen. Quick-fix methods in my field of psychology come and go like seasonal birds. Medication is the current panacea for our anxiety and depression, but it is too often prescribed without the necessary therapeutic support required to reach the deep under-standing necessary for meaningful change. While we purport to fight drug addiction, we are assaulted with ads for prescription drugs on our television screens. Prescription drugs now rival street drugs in popularity.

These problems can seem overwhelming. Yet if each one of us who feels overwhelmed and disempowered were to say, "I refuse to live like this and I'm going to do something about it," a great tide of energy would be unleashed that would bring change and carry humanity forward to the potential for greatness that is our birthright. There would be a great rebirth for all of us on the planet!

We humans are a work in progress, and you and I have a potentially significant part to play in the solution to the problems we all face. Our problems, even the massive environmental ones, are caused by ignorance. And ignorance can be eradicated. That's what evolution is all about. Our human history is the story of facing and dealing with adversity and ignorance. The time to join forces for the common good is always *now*.

This requires an understanding of our interdependence. When humans lack the sense of connection to the whole that must be present to motivate ethical behavior, they tend to let their own selfish, shortsighted interests blind them to the effects they have on the world around them. In fact, what the unethical person most often demonstrates could be called *situational ethics*, which is little more than a disguised *lack* of ethics. Several examples, familiar to all, come immediately to mind. While Hitler may have been kind and loving to his mistress, he was unspeakably evil in his dealings with millions of people. Even the late dictator of Iraq, Saddam Hussein, had a daughter who saw her father as loving and kind, despite the fact that he had her husband assassinated! Our own former President, Bill Clinton, undoubtedly a charismatic leader and doting father, scandalized his watch in the White House by dallying with a young woman close to his daughter's age and lying about it on national television.

Ethics are not something you put on and take off as it serves your purposes. Quick-fix attempts are feeble at best because they only handle the symptoms and fail to get at the real cause of decay. Those who are unethical may act one way at home and another in the world. An ethical person demonstrates the same level of integrity in the boardroom as in the bedroom. An ethical person contributes to the whole world just by acting with integrity in his or her own home and community.

Refuse to play the victim; stop looking for someone to blame and figure out how *you* can make a difference. That's power at the personal level, where it must be experienced by each of us. Your willingness to be in action gives you an immediate experience of the personal power available to you. When you are in action, it opens up your sense of connection to both your True Self and the world. This sense of connection is the wellspring of personal integrity, which both springs from and develops into a desire to be ethical. An ethical person in turn creates a climate of stability and security by displaying the same integrity wherever he or she is: at home, at work, with friend or with foe. This radical integrity is personal power at work! It is a powerful force for good in the world.

Your Journey to Radical Integrity

"Fulfilling your highest potential actually means acting on your highest and deepest truth each moment of your life."
—Caroline Myss

While you can't (and really don't need to) change the whole world, you *can* change you. When *you* change, others are affected because they will have to relate to you differently. You can clean up *your* attitude, *your* act, *your* environment. In your small corner of the world, you can create the peace and harmony that creates a deeply personal experience of stability, trust, and safety. And all of this starts with the smallest unit—the family.

Ethics must be woven into the fabric of each person's life during the process of enculturation, education, and maturation at the most personal level, the family.

This ethical dilemma can be solved in your family because that's where values are learned. It's as simple as that. The family, where you learn the basic set of beliefs and behaviors that provide both your world-view and the guideposts for life, is where ethics are imparted. If the family you are born into is healthy and strong, morally sound with values that nurture the best in its members, you can indeed count your blessings. It's very likely that you will mature into what psychologist Abraham Maslow, who is probably most well known for his Hierarchy of Needs, calls a "fully-functional person." This means you have the ability to utilize your gifts and have a sense of purpose. You will go out into the world knowing how to create an ethical life because you have the self-esteem necessary for living with integrity.

If you weren't born into such a family, if instead your family was neglectful, abusive, and lacking in the ethical behavior that nurtures its members, you will have to overcome many obstacles in order to fulfill the potential you were born with. Simply put, because you haven't learned what integrity looks like and feels like because you didn't grow up with it around you, you will have trouble knowing what it looks or feels like to live ethically. You may follow the rules out of fear, but you won't experience the power that comes from knowing the importance of trust and choosing to have integrity. People who have integrity may even cause you discomfort.

After years of living as a single mother, finishing two graduate degrees, and raising my children alone, I knew the importance of family. I knew its good side and I knew its bad. I learned so much that was worthwhile in my family, including the value of nature, beauty, art, music, and intellectual stimulation, but I had also been deeply wounded by my parents' unhappy marriage, my father's alcoholism and sexual abuse, and my mother's insecurity, insensitivity, and lack of emotional closeness. With much effort and determination, I was willing to change my thinking and evaluate my behavior. I have experienced the deep joy that comes from knowing that these trials and tribulations can be overcome and accepted as just a part of life. I now see that my wounds helped me to grow, like the sand in the oyster shell that produces a pearl. Your wounds contain the same potential for beauty and power. I have been honed, challenge by challenge, to grow and embody my potential. You are being challenged to do the same. That's what makes life worthwhile. I know it's never too late to do this and because I believe it, I see it everywhere I go!

True Adults

"The self is not something that one finds. It is something that one creates."
—Thomas Szasz

The main reason that humans don't know how to function as moral, ethical, nurturing parents to the children they bring into the world is that they haven't learned how to be what I call "True Adults." They are functioning like little children in big bodies, using the beliefs and behaviors that they saw their parents display (or they are stuck in rebellion against their parents, doing the opposite of what their parents did while stubbornly refusing to see what they're doing). As Alberto Villoldo expresses in *Illumination,* "The birth rite does not happen automatically when we pass through the birth canal. It was orchestrated by parents who refuse to look at their children as mere extensions of themselves. If the child does not rebel against this version of reality, he'll be stuck trying to please his parents or perpetually rebelling against them." Mistakenly, parents assume that because their bodies have matured, they are adults. These parents have grown up, but they aren't True Adults—mature, whole people. Furthermore, they aren't prepared to parent children in an empowering way.

The fear and alienation, destruction and disturbance, cynicism and despair we witness in the world can be traced to the immature, dysfunctional, unexamined beliefs and behaviors we learn in our families and then take out into the world with us, repeating the dysfunctional patterns from generation to generation.

As a society, we've tried to remedy the situation by legislating morality and ethics from the far-off halls of government, but those laws are not enough to alter the deep familial foundations from which integrity, morality, and ethics spring. Seeing the lack of ethics that corporate leaders and politicians display only increases our sense of frustration and helplessness. While that outer focus allows us to avoid our own shortcomings, projecting our dysfunctions and character defects onto others is not the solution. We may look at others as the problem and still feel blameless and innocent, but this doesn't solve anything. In fact, it even adds to the problem by perpetuating victim consciousness—the belief that we are essentially powerless to change our lives. We learn this powerlessness in our families, and it is here that we can correct the problem.

In the ancient wise words of *The I Ching,* "When the family is in order, all of society is in order." Our families are *not* in order; our history is about the struggle that families have experienced as they dealt with the prevailing ignorance of the day. Historians speak of an agrarian society, where families worked together in the fields and farms. The health of those families may well be overromanticized. Certainly since the start of the Industrial Revolution, when fathers left the home to go to work in the factories, women have had to bear the brunt of child rearing. Fathers were sperm-donors and mothers were left to assume the major responsibility of raising children. Fathers were even seen as unnecessary to a child's development other than for occasional discipline and steady financial support. Luckily, that is gradually changing as the roles of males and females shift because both parents are probably working.

Nevertheless, there is still ignorance about the importance of the role that fathers play; children are still left without a balanced perspective of the feminine and the masculine. My father was powerless in our home. His pat answer was, "Go ask your mother." He took no part in child rearing and wasn't expected to assume one. I had friends whose mothers were powerless and waited for Daddy to come home and whip the kids into shape. Neither model gives children the nurturing they need.

I am excited to see that crucial imbalance in the roles of men and women being corrected in many families today as more men share in child rearing. We are learning that raising children is a cooperative venture where fathers and mothers must be willing to share the power, rather than simply enforce the rules. Gabrielle Roth speaks of the symbolic roles that parents must be willing to play in her fascinating book, *Maps to Ecstasy*:

> *The mother embodies the feminine instincts of nurturing and receptivity. Her sacred role is to teach her baby how to be in a body, respect her baby's uniqueness and nurture its self-worth. When a mother forgets her sacred function, it is destructive for herself, her child, her society and her world. Far from being unimportant, the father embodies the masculine instinct of dynamic creativity. It is his role to pass on the instinctive ability to relate appropriately to others, teaching loyalty, companionship, sharing and fairness. Your relationship to your father determines whether you can be*

yourself and express your heart or whether you must achieve, perform, charm, seduce, compete, please, demand, negate or even destroy to feel recognized.

My own children have struggled with both of their parents because we did not understand attachment and how truly vital we were to their development. They are still trying to reestablish a good relationship with their father, who left town when I divorced him. They struggle with me because I was ill-equipped to be both breadwinner and sole parent, trying to get my own needs met and not knowing what that looked like. I feel sad about all they've gone through without the benefit of having both a mature father and a mother on a daily basis. Yet I feel hopeful, because their father and I have both been willing to face our own parents' immaturity and lack of mature modeling. Rather than act blameless, we have apologized to our children for our failures in raising them into mature adulthood.

What you and I *can* change is our own personal lives. Dealing with our own personal and family issues with radical integrity is what can empower us.

To make these internal personal changes, you can begin by looking at *your own* integrity and the values you are committed to in your family and community, the smaller units that create our world. Are you an enforcer of your own perspective of the world, or is there room for everyone's perspective within a shared responsibility for *everyone's* welfare? Integrity involves a deep respect for both self and others; when it's "us against them," somebody has to lose and that loser is not going to be a productive member of any group. Bucky Fuller devoted his life to integrity because he believed it was the most important thing necessary to ensure the survival of our species. Each of us has a part to play in uplifting humanity through our personal commitment to integrity, to living ethical and moral lives. That is a radical act in a time that worships the gods of materialism ("I'm going to get mine!") and victim consciousness. It is the radical act that can bring peace and harmony to us all.

In *The Isaiah Effect*, Gregg Braden's account of visiting the abbot of a Tibetan monastery, he tells of ancient teachings that can provide the necessary foundation for bringing solace and healing to our modern world. The abbot says, "Peace is of the greatest importance in our world today. In the absence of peace, we lose what we have gained. In the presence of peace, all things are possible: love, compassion, and forgiveness. Peace is the source of all things. I would ask the people of the world to find peace in *themselves*, so that their peace may be mirrored in the world."

Alberto Villoldo says, "When you claim your own separate identity, you claim your right to your dreams and stop holding others responsible for your choices. Then you discover your genuine power, the power of inner peace."

An identity grounded in personal integrity is necessary for self-esteem. Self-esteem creates an inner peace that can withstand the turbulence of the world.

Peaceful people have integrity; they are ethical people. A human must be ethical to experience peace and harmony. That, in turn, is how we contribute peace and harmony to the world. Peace and harmony start with you and me being responsible for what we believe and how we act wherever we are. That is the practice of ethics.

Our culture is failing in its sacred trust to impart ethics as a part of the natural order to its people. This sacred trust must begin with childhood. How to impart these ethics should be a priority for all of us. It will necessitate examining your own personal beliefs and behaviors and it will also require a willingness to actually do things differently, facing your own discomfort and complacency. While it seems we humans often must be pushed off the ledge before we will do the deep work of real change, hopefully, events in the recent past have motivated us to take the leap!

We need a new model for adulthood that conveys the information people need for parenting children at every level of their being, physical, emotional, and mental. This new model must acknowledge the multidimensionality of human beings and meet their needs on *each* of those dimensions. The new model must be clear about what children need at each dimension and committed to meeting those needs with caring, nurturing, loving behaviors. People who understand this new model will be capable of parenting children so they grow up and contribute their gifts with a true sense of purpose, without a lot of handicaps, fears, and dysfunctional behaviors to overcome. This means that parents must learn what it means to be a True Adult.

Ethics, integrity, and morality are all words that True Adults embody; you need to *learn* this from your family.

True Adults are willing to examine assumptions, beliefs, and behaviors that were inherited from others as they grew up. True Adulthood involves a willingness to choose mature behaviors that respond to life in ethical ways that honor the interdependence of us all. You must coexist with your fellow man in order to thrive. You must be able to trust others, feeling safe and supported by your fellow man, if you are to have a meaningful life. This requires that you act with integrity in your dealings with others.

Imparting Integrity

"Inherently, each one of us has the substance within to achieve whatever our goals and dreams define. What is missing from each of us is the training, education, knowledge, and insight to utilize what we already have."
—Mark Twain

In order to change the future, you need to get clear about how the past created the present. That provides the knowledge and insight so essential for achieving your goals. Children use the grown-ups in their lives as models. If their models are not truly adult, they have no images or experiences about how to become a True Adult. It's as simple as that.

No matter what our circumstances, we all have one thing in common: the maturation process we go through called childhood and adolescence. We humans are a product of the enculturation done to us by other humans when we were innocent, unformed children. We are living in a cultural sea of beliefs and assumptions about reality (a paradigm) that informs and shapes our experiences. From the moment of conception, we are exposed to conditions that either further or hinder our development into loving, compassionate, capable, creative, wise, and peaceful adults (the very qualities that True Adults display).

My own life is an example that gives ample evidence to my point. I have been through numerous abusive mate relationships. While I may have been unhappy, I now understand that I was "comfortable" with them. (Since I was molested as a very young child, abuse feels "normal" or familiar to me.) It has taken me a lifetime to get comfortable with *safe* men, a sad but true dilemma in my own life (and one shared by far too many people, as I have learned). You learn in your family to see the world as either safe or unsafe. That world-view is in place by the age of seven, stored as information in your brain that affects everything you see and do. As you mature, things that don't fit your world-view are avoided, rejected, or simply not noticed. You even become comfortable with things that are actually *unsafe*—it's "just the way it is" and you will accept that familiar energy into your life, even though it makes you very unhappy.

Ethics are the natural result of being surrounded and guided by ethical people, people with integrity.

Just as dishonesty is actually learned, so are ethics. Children naturally *want* to do the right thing (to be authentic, morally sound, and respectful of self and others), but they need guidance to know what the right thing is. They weren't born with an ethics guidebook, but they do *want* to be "good" (i.e., please their parents) and will be if encouraged by parents who act ethically. On the other hand, if the parents do not value ethics, children have a hard time learning to value it. They copy their parents' behavior. This causes a lot of confusion for them when they start school, as any teacher can tell you.

The type of family children come from is readily apparent to any teacher. Children from unethical, immoral families clash with children from a different kind of family. Bullying is a serious outcome of this clash, and schools can be a very scary place because of that! It has reached a crisis point, because too many adults look the other way while bullying is going on. We have become a very detached society and it hurts all of us. We will walk right by people who are being harmed by others, as many studies have shown. Human beings need connection; detachment should be an option when privacy is desired, not an avoidance of moral duty in the face of obvious harm.

The Unseen World

"The mind projects what it believes and we try to change the screen instead of the projector."
—Byron Katie

When ethics are not present in the family, children grow up without a moral compass. When parents lack integrity, they create families that are unsafe, dysfunctional, abusive, and immoral (all of which are unethical). That experience becomes the child's world-view, or reality, as it were. This world-view is based on fear. These fearful experiences come to be *expected* and this "expectation of disaster" becomes a part of their perception of life. You actually *expect* the worst and don't understand that it is your expectation that attracts the negative energy!

Like energy attracts like energy; that is a universal law that is always operating in the unseen world, even though things may look entirely the opposite in the seen world (where we experience that *opposites attract*, like magnets). This makes for a very confusing experience for humans. What seems to be true at one level is actually untrue at another. In other words, the laws that apply to the physical world are different from the laws that apply to the non-physical, which is a much larger part of reality!

A True Adult is willing to expand his or her awareness to include both the seen and the unseen worlds, acknowledging that truth is contained in the paradoxical union of *both* worlds.

When a fear-based and very limited perception learned from immature, unaware parents is projected out onto the larger community and world as the child matures, the results can be predicted. I think this is expressed well in the Bible: "As you reap, so shall you sow."

Wise people have been telling us for centuries that our lives actually occur as a self-fulfilling prophecy that mirrors both our positive and our negative expectations. As the Buddha said long ago in *The Dhammapada*, "We are what we think. All that we are arises with our thoughts. With our thoughts we create the world." Quantum physics has shown us that, indeed, the world does show up as we expect it to. Or as Wayne Dyer says, "You've got to *believe* it to see it."

Expecting the world to be a fearful, dangerous place and the resulting painful emotions is the root cause of all psychological disorders, including addiction and depression, and the wide variety of sociopathic and psychopathic disorders. A world-view formed by fear and shame incurred during the years when maturation and enculturation were taking place will not include the ethical beliefs and behaviors necessary for developing the self-esteem that contributes to creating a safe and sane world.

Growing Up

"Until you have done the healing of any family dysfunctions, you will unconsciously recreate your childhood dysfunction wherever you go in order to resolve the issues."
—Harville Hendrix

Children's "business" is to pay attention to what's going on. They are excellent at their jobs.

Parents get the full attention of their children; that's how they figure out how to deal with this world they have come into as vulnerable, innocent, immature, uninformed, and totally dependent small people. Their play reflects what they are observing in their environment; they "act out" what they see. Too many children today are suffering from an epidemic of obesity, learning disabilities and depression, bullying and violence. They see too much of this and act it out as they mature. Is this something to be alarmed about? I think so!

Today children grow up with the whole world in their living room. They are exposed at younger and younger ages to a far larger and more complicated world through the eyes of the media. Much of what they see is far from ethical; it is scary and confusing. When violence and ugliness happen across the world, they see it the same day, sometimes the same hour. They watch people being killed on a daily basis. In fact, violence is now exciting to many children, rather than scary the way it was to me as a child. (I still can't watch horror movies!) Even if children live in functional, nurturing families, they are exposed daily to a world that is far from that!

When I was a kid I loved Westerns. I knew the good guys would always win. But it's hard to tell who the good guys are any more. People put on such a good act, it's hard to know whom or what to trust. Getting away with being unethical is even seen as "cool." On the other hand, we are exposed to all the "dirt" about everybody. Everybody is twittering about everybody else. Advertising and the media certainly give thoughtful people reason to be depressed, to despair that ethics, integrity, morality, and virtue have become a mockery in our modern world. Our idea of the good life has become materialistic, self-absorbed, and empty, detached from genuine relationship to others and to nature.

Countless children experience parents who are preoccupied with work and their own lives. The television provides the main modeling for these children. By the time they become teens, they are more interested in their latest idol than in their own families. Because of the increasing dependence on television and computers, it's easy to grow up watching life instead of living it. Couple this with parents who both work and we have a situation that makes children feel lonely and alienated, lacking a sense of connection to anyone or anything. It's way too easy and inviting for children to stay detached from the world today. Their attachment is to cell phones and pictures on a screen, not to people!

Too many politicians are out of integrity and too many governments are corrupt. Militiamen gather weapons to protect themselves from our government while children carry guns to school to protect themselves from each other and teachers they are angry with. Children watch us sacrifice our health and well-being, even sell our souls for material goods, while huge numbers of people go to sleep hungry, homeless, and sick. While drowning in the garbage left over from our wastefulness, we agonize over our credit card debt and worry about having enough money. We continue to reject those who are different from us, as our own struggle with civil rights demonstrates.

Too many people on this planet treat the water, the soil, and other resources of our planet with the same incredible disrespect they show their fellow humans. Vast numbers of women are relegated to a lower status and deemed unworthy of equal pay with their male counterparts; in some nations, they are no more than chattel. Slavery is still practiced and children are sold for prostitution here in our midst. Even in the best neighborhoods, children worry about being abducted.

Children take this on as "reality," absorbing it into a very scary world-view. What an incredibly painful view of the world our children are inheriting! No wonder they want to detach, to escape (just like many of the adults they know). This is fertile ground for addiction, and very few children grow up without some kind of compulsive activity or substance (or both) that they need in order to keep away the gnawing anxiety that something is wrong and the fear that it's *them*. You were born narcissistic for a reason: to focus on the tasks of maturing without being unduly distracted. But if that narcissism is not respected with a corresponding response from adults who assist you in mastering the tasks of childhood, you never outgrow the nagging feeling that you're the cause of everything.

Well, you are and you aren't, and that paradox requires a mature mind that has gotten its needs for attachment met.

Empowering Children

"Healthy parenting allows children to grow into an adult who is congruent, the same person inside as out."
—J. Keith Miller

As if the media world weren't depressing enough, children have to deal with the prevalent disrespectful and dangerous assumption that they need to be controlled, managed, punished, and otherwise shaped and molded because they are not "good enough." Rather than question our notions of what it means to be "good," we have turned the doctrine of Original Sin into a manifesto for mistreating children. Our current paradigm about children sees them as flawed and disregards their innocence, vulnerability, and narcissism. (My mother's mantra was that I was selfish, which made it incredibly difficult for me to know what I wanted or needed at all! She sent me on my honeymoon with my second husband by reminding him of that.) Failing to understand that we learn to be ethical by being treated ethically, we persist in raising children with the belief that they need fixing. Then we punish them for meeting our negative expectations, believing we are justified in our unethical treatment of children. And then we wonder why they have no self-esteem!

Children are one of the favorite scapegoats in our culture and we don't see the damage we're doing. Blaming children for the problems that occur in our families and schools is one of the most immature and damaging things that goes on in our culture. It is highly unethical!

Furthermore, as you mature, our culture imposes an *outer focus* on you that forces you to give up the *inner focus* of self-inspection and self-reflection so necessary for the development of self-esteem, integrity, and a code of ethics. Daydreaming, the child's way of inner focus, is done by all children but punished by most adults. By the time you hit adolescence, although your body has matured enough to undertake adult responsibilities, you have lost touch with your essential nature. Too many people have matured physically, but are lonely and alienated from their real selves, from others, and especially from their sacredness. This alienation creates confusion and insecurity, which they then bring into their adult life. Some of us know this. (I was never good at denying my pain; I used to wish I were better at being phony.) Sadly, too many are totally unconscious of their deep fears and insecurities. My experience has been that many people just cover them up with a good act and hope others buy it. In fact, many people do buy into the act, in an unconscious, unspoken agreement: "I won't notice your pain if you ignore mine." (Also, let me say I am acutely aware that if you're reading this, you may be one of those who really strives to be authentic, which is a true gift to the world.)

Our schools are a reflection of the same paradigm seen in our families. Too many educators see children as the problem. (All it takes is *one* insensitive teacher to damage a vulnerable child—mean teachers leave an indelible mark that only safe, protective, mature parents can help erase.) Children require safety to develop their potential, yet too often schools are not very safe places. They are places where children are seen as needing to be controlled and where children get punished for behaviors they have learned by watching the adults around them. Children are exposed to pettiness, insecurity, jealousy, meanness, control dramas, and a variety of other immature, power-abusing behaviors displayed by the adults who are their models, both at home and at school. And these immature teachers are protected by the tenure system. I've spent too many years in schools, both as a teacher and as a parent, to deny that children's behavior can be atrocious, but the fact remains that so-called "adults" have created the environment that children are reacting against. No wonder carrying a weapon feels good to some of these disempowered, distraught, neglected, and abused children. They see no other way to feel safe in an environment that feels so hostile.

Too many parents have abdicated their role to the schools, dedicating their time to pursuing materialistic goals, and leaving the school to bring up their children. Schools are not prepared for parenting, and children get lost in the void. Even in the best of scenarios, education does not guarantee we will become True Adults. I have a lot of education and, while it was valuable, it was not enough to make me one. It certainly did not make me a better parent. Despite a degree in education and child development, I was still at the mercy of unconscious beliefs and behaviors (taken on in preschool years) that controlled too much of the way I was as a parent. In fact, I parented very much the way my mother did, with some rebelling against things that made me angry enough to challenge, but ignorant about far too many things that were incredibly important.

Our institutions, corporations, and professional settings are the scene of replays of the childish behavior and unresolved childhood wounds we took on as children. I consulted with a large bank in New York City and saw in corporate executives some of the most childish behaviors I've ever witnessed! Sadly, we've watched as these immature, petty, and unethical behaviors reveal themselves, even in the most intelligent, well-educated people. (Our recent bank failures and corporate scandals are a perfect example.) It is always delightful to meet someone who appears to be authentic and mature, but it's not uncommon for people who know how to *act* in a reasonably mature manner to eventually end up revealing their agenda, which is to manipulate and control those around them. These control dramas can reach epic heights in the corporate world, as witnessed by the deep lack of corporate ethics that our current recession is revealing.

As a society, we worship at the altar of intelligence while ignoring the other multidimensional factors that create a fully functioning adult. These include the need for real security and safety, the ability to feel and express emotions appropriately, a personal connection to the sacred, the willingness to take responsibility for our own health, and the commitment to treating others and ourselves with respect and dignity. Actually, very few people lack an acceptable degree of intelligence. However, without maturity and without a connection to the heart, intelligence can end up being used in destructive ways.

Perfectly smart people learn immature behaviors well and continue them on into their adult years, contaminating their quality of life and teaching them to the next generation.

The sad truth is that *as a society*, we are childish at worst, adolescent at best. As a result, we as a society suffer from low self-esteem, often covered up by grandiosity.

Without models of True Adults to emulate, children are at the mercy of childish modeling. What you learn to call being "adult" is actually *playacting your idea of an adult,* much like you did as a kid. This *idea* (or perception) of "adult" is based on your experience of your parents. If they weren't truly mature, then your perception of what being an adult looks like tends to be immature also. In fact, it pretty much matches your parents' idea of it; or it is the opposite, which isn't any more mature and is just being stuck in rebelling.

In other words, you remain childish, but *pretend* you're adult after your body gets big, much the way you played "grown-up" as a child. Cased in a grown-up body, you still think and act like a kid—feeling disempowered and defensive, not because you *want* to be, but because you still experience yourself as powerless and live in the fear that you *need* to defend yourself. If you *know* you feel powerless, you act inferior; if you don't know it, you act grandiose. But they're flip sides of the same childish, disempowered coin.

Looking in the Mirror

"Integrity without knowledge is weak and useless, and knowledge without integrity is dangerous and dreadful."
—Samuel Johnson

Our world is in desperate need of more True Adults. Our culture's failure to understand and support your multidimensional unfolding into an authentic, empowered being leaves you without accurate information or tools to fully mature and utilize your gifts. Instead, our culture rewards braininess and the repression of emotions. It worships beauty and supports addictive behaviors, such as workaholism and codependence. It promotes a childish spirituality, teaching that you are separate from God and therefore reliant upon someone more elevated in purity and stature to intercede on your lowly behalf. It too often teaches conformity, rewards compliance, and punishes challenges to authority (unless you happen to be rich enough to get away with being an oddball nonconformist!).

Where do these beliefs about children come from? Why do some adults choose to act unethically? Why do parents who love their children and want the best for them fail to empower those children to become ethical adults? To answer these questions, you must be willing to ask some tough questions and look at some uncomfortable, even painful assumptions. If you don't challenge your assumptions about adulthood, about children and child rearing, chances are that you will just keep doing to the next generation more of what damaged you.

It takes a great deal of maturity to look in the mirror that children provide and focus on changing *yourself* instead of making children or others the problem. Too many parents and teachers want their children to get help, get medicated, be controlled and modified, but are unwilling to be accountable for their own part in creating the children's problems. We resist feeling the discomfort and shame that comes from examining what we are doing to children that prevents them from maturing. We have huge levels of denial about how abusive we actually are to children (not to mention to each other!). We resist taking responsibility for our own lack of integrity and for the fact that we actually *teach* children to be disrespectful and to blame others, especially those smaller and weaker. Every bully is a disrespected, needy child acting out his pain!

We can stop the cycle of decay in our families. You can begin with you—by examining your beliefs and behaviors and changing *them* rather than trying to "fix" children. Children are our teachers as much as we are theirs, and some of us have not been very good students. You can begin by becoming a good student.

Examining Assumptions

"To change the conditions that allow war, oppression and mass suffering, we must change the thinking that has allowed the conditions to be present. To know peace in our world, we must become peace in our lives."
—Gregg Braden

The current dysfunctional environment we create for children actually prevents the natural unfolding of a consciously integrated sense of self as a multidimensional being. A being who is empowered to create a sense of place and purpose in the world, has a sense of his or her own worth, and is safely and securely connected to his or her body and emotions is prepared to function responsibly, maturely, and ethically as a True Adult.

Despite the popularity of self-help books and the emergence of therapy as a tool for self-improvement, you may still struggle with the same old assumptions and problems your parents and their parents faced—a prevalent attitude that "if it was good enough for me, it's good enough for my kids." Well, it's not!

Our current parenting paradigm is dysfunctional. Below I have listed the deeply embedded beliefs and behaviors that make up this paradigm. I've been in some kind of therapy most of my life; my own children and the people I work with are still dealing with the effects of this paradigm. As you read through it, be willing to examine whether you experienced some or all of this:

CURRENT (DYSFUNCTIONAL) PARENTING PARADIGM

1. Lack of a deep connection with and trust for children

Parents often fail to let their children attach to them as babies and young children. If you weren't attached to your parents, you will need to learn about attachment. Your parents probably weren't properly attached when they were young and may not have been treated with respect and kindness by their own parents. Unattached parents end up with trust issues and lack an understanding of the damage that was done to them, and therefore the ability to attach to their own children. Children require attachment with parents who see them, feel them, and talk with them in a close personal manner, and who believe in their worth and demonstrate that with respect and loving kindness.

2. Ignorance about multidimensional needs and the developmental stages of childhood, coupled with the substitution of material goods for real emotional needs

We live in an extremely materialistic culture, in which many children are emotionally and physically deprived. They have toys and computers, watch TV, and have a very busy schedule, but lack the presence of their parents' full attention and affection. They often eat a diet that is full of empty calories and sweets; they are too sedentary. Parents may assume that what they got from their parents is good enough for their own children; or they may struggle to give their children all the things they felt deprived of, not understanding that these "things" weren't what they really needed.

Parents need to be willing to get educated about parenting and childhood developmental needs. They need to understand that material things are not a substitute for physical, emotional, and mental fulfillment.

3. Expectations that it is the children's job is to make their parents feel happy, comfortable, and fulfilled

Parents do not have a right to use their child to meet their physical, emotional, or mental needs. The parents' job is to meet their child's needs and find other adults to meet their own needs. If the parents' marriage is not providing for their physical, emotional, and mental needs, they need to seek professional marriage counseling. Otherwise, the child will be drawn into a surrogate spouse relationship with the parent, an extremely difficult and debilitating scenario for a child and one that is very hard to resist because the child needs the parent. Children should not fulfill spouse roles for their parents! I see an enormous number of people who were their parent's surrogate spouse. I recognize them because I was one also! It's like being emotionally married to your parent, and it makes having your own mate very difficult.

4. Use of blame, punishment, and control to manage children

Blame, punishment, and control create fear and shame in children. Children do not require managing like a project; they need healthy attachment. They require attention, affection, genuine interest, and feedback from their parents, not managing. They need to be allowed to experiment within boundaries and under their parents' watchful eyes. Parents need to be willing to look at the reasons why their child's behavior upsets them by examining their own history and working out their own issues with competent help from professionals. If necessary, parents need to relearn the power of being treated with dignity and respect and break the cycle of abuse and/or neglect that may have been handed down from generations past.

5. Assumptions that because you're a grown-up, you are mature and know what is best for children

Adulthood is not just a physical phenomenon. Unless and until you have examined your own childhood and the ways that your parents wounded you, you will unconsciously recreate these wounds with your own children and in your marriage. You will continue to act childishly, even though your body is mature. True Adulthood requires an examination of *all* beliefs, assumptions, and behaviors. True Adults *choose* their beliefs and behaviors after this examination. Be willing to get educated about healthy parenting if you are going to have a child. Be willing to learn how to be a True Adult, honoring your multidimensional nature with integrity.

6. Use of children to work out the parents' own unresolved conflicts and wounds

You can be sure you will unconsciously re-create your own childhood wounds. Your self-concept was formed *at an early age* from what your parents told you and how they acted. It needs updating! Problems with your child probably mean you and your mate have problems; having integrity means considering this possibility. Look at your own issues and resolve them with professional help, if necessary. Refuse to pass on your unresolved wounds. Do whatever it takes to truly attach to and enjoy your child, also accepting that all humans have bad days. You don't need to be perfect, just committed to doing the best you can. Stop acting as though you never do anything wrong; apologize and do it better next time! Let your child teach you.

7. Lack of parental integrity ("Do as I say, not as I do.")

Refrain from asking your child to do anything that you don't do yourself. Don't ask your child to stop swearing if you do. Don't ask your children not to smoke if you do. Children will model after what you *do*, not what you *say*. It makes them angry when they get old enough to realize you aren't doing what you told them to do. This leads to rebellion and acting out their unexpressed anger and frustration (or turning to self-destructive behaviors). Your children deserve the best of you in order to have the best chance of being all they can be!

8. Interpretation of love as care-taking, worry, and pity

Our model of love is very codependent, based on the above-mentioned qualities. That's not love; it's codependence and it's abusive. Arthur Aron of Stony Brook University calls love a *motivational state* that leads to various emotions ranging from euphoria to misery. It can allow us to melt the boundaries between each other and experience a deep communion with others. But it can also cause enormous pain when we choose harmful behaviors. So the powerful motivational state of love offers us the opportunity to make choices to refrain from any behavior that leads to harming another person. Any behavior that is not loving and kind, that has an underlying motive that is disrespectful and abusive, does deep damage to children. Get educated about love; acknowledge that we all have a lot to learn. Help your children learn how to function as adults, step by step, and trust that they want to grow into functional people and will do so if they have a model of how it looks and feels. You are the model. Have radical integrity and accept the responsibility for modeling real love.

9. Encouraging children to remain dependent to fill the parents' inner emptiness

Children learn how to give when they have parents who demonstrate giving. Too many adults *take* from their children, using them to meet needs that their children cannot fulfill. Adults need to fill their own needs with other assenting adults. They need to face what isn't working in their marriages and stop expecting their children to pick up the slack. Seek marriage counseling or go on a retreat with the partner who has grown distant and find out what it will take to reconnect. Adults need to be willing to let their children go when they have matured instead of keeping them close in order to fill their own loneliness. Failing to do this is damaging to both child and parent. It prevents children from successfully forming their own mate relationships.

10. Blaming children for the problems of the parents and the family

Parents are the models, and they need to look at the mirror their children provide for clues about the effectiveness of their parenting. Children live what they learn. If children are treated with consistency, respect, and loving kindness, they will be cooperative. If a child isn't cooperative, instead of blaming the child, parents need to be willing to search for the cause of the behavior, including themselves and others in the child's environment. Then they need to respect the child's right to express his or her feelings and model an appropriate way to do that. As a nation, we are emotionally ignorant and crippled. Take responsibility for healing that part of your life.

This paradigm contains the roots of the decay in our families and in our communities that create fear and shame in children and prevent them from maturing. Children want and need their parents' love and they will sacrifice

themselves to get it. It is shameful for parents to let this happen.

The truth is that there isn't a single behavior in this paradigm that is *truly* adult. None of this paradigm demonstrates integrity. Take a moment to notice if you feel insulted about this, because if it hit home with you, you now have an opportunity to begin your own healing process. Feeling righteous indignation is actually a defense against feeling ashamed, the most painful of all feelings and one that most of us avoid at any cost. Avoiding shame doesn't work; neither does wallowing in it. Facing it and making the necessary changes can heal shame.

You don't need to carry shame for doing what all humans instinctively do—embrace their culture's paradigm. What you do need is a healthy dose of compassion and the intention to have radical integrity, coupled with the willingness to examine and change your attitudes and behaviors. Doing this creates a space for you to let go of the shame. Chances are most of us didn't do anything maliciously. (If you did, then amends are definitely in order!) If you've been acting on malicious feelings, seek professional help to deal with your own anger.

Upon examination, you can see that while this paradigm may be the best notion of dealing with children we've come up with thus far, you now have an opportunity to take a good look at the false assumptions about children and the ignorance about real human needs that they reflect.

Here's how to examine false assumptions:

1. You must realize that your assumptions about children and adults are based on ignorant, incomplete, sometimes false notions that you took on unconsciously just by living in this culture.

Reinforcing these assumptions is your obsession with fitting in and being accepted, a normal childhood need that too few outgrow. Enculturation encourages you to think the way others think without wondering if it really reflects the truth. Furthermore, you may have been punished for challenges to authority and to the status quo. Unaware of how you made assumptions about the world based on the paradigm you were born into, you ended up doing what you saw others doing without questioning why. This is normal human behavior that we all need to challenge.

2. You need to make a distinction between a "grown-up" and an "adult."

A grown-up has a mature body, but it's a serious mistake to assume that's all there is to being an adult. My trusty old dictionary defines *adult* as "one grown to full size and strength; mature." The definition of *mature* is "brought by natural process to completeness of growth and development; of or pertaining to a condition of full development." This definition doesn't make our multidimensionality clear. While we have assumed that physical maturity makes an adult, it actually defines a "grown-up." There is much more to an adult; after your body matures, it is your responsibility to challenge your own thinking, your own emotional expression, and your perceptions of reality.

3. You have to challenge your notion of what adulthood is in the following ways:

> **a. Adulthood is not a given; it is actually determined by the *maturity* of the set of learned beliefs and behaviors you assimilated from your caretakers and our cultural paradigm.**

These beliefs and behaviors may or may not be mature, depending upon what you learned as a child. They have little to do with size or stature, intelligence, or social status and everything to do with your *personal experience* of the people who raised you. To the extent that your models for adulthood were, in fact, immature, you will struggle with the tasks of adulthood, at both a personal and professional level. To the extent that you learned how to live in healthy, loving, ethical, and responsible ways from your caretakers, you matured into a functional, responsible, and independent adult, capable of maintaining interdependent, ethical, and fulfilling relationships with others, both personally and professionally. You have radical integrity.

> **b. Adulthood is a journey, an evolving process that involves an *ongoing* commitment to examining all assumptions and to utilizing all your multidimensional capacities to their fullest potential.**

Adulthood is not a destination, a place you get to when your body matures. You are much more than a body with a personality. You are a complex *multidimensional* being that functions not only physically, but perceptually, emotionally, mentally, and spiritually. Your body may have matured, but if the rest of you (the other dimensions) has not, you are *not* a truly mature adult. Maturity is a journey that requires a deep desire to fulfill one's multidimensional potential, coupled with a commitment to the regular ongoing examination of all beliefs and behaviors with the intention of taking *full responsibility* for one's thoughts, feelings, and actions. This responsibility for one's actions requires the conscious choice to use one's power for *generating* life rather than destroying life. These choices happen on a daily basis, in big ways and small ways.

> **c. To the extent that you are able and willing to *choose* to act with integrity and accountability, you are a mature and therefore ethical, empowered adult.**

If you have not *fully* matured, perceptually, emotionally, mentally, and spiritually, you are not prepared to deal with the choices that inevitably and inexorably assault you throughout your life. To the extent that you were given a perspective of fear, shame, and powerlessness, you will struggle with feeling a sense of personal power and with assuming the tasks of adulthood. You will end up re-creating your childhood dysfunctions, resorting to defenses to cover up your pain and shame, and struggling with consistently maintaining responsibility or behaving ethically. Make a commitment to yourself to learn about the ways you need to mature, practice these new behaviors, and let a trusted friend hold you accountable for doing so. Then give yourself the rest of your life to practice!

d. You *can* create and embrace a better model for adulthood and for raising children. You can *impart* ethics to your children so we don't need to *legislate* it when they become adults. It is the most important task before all of us in this century!

One of the main benefits we stand to gain from changing the current parenting paradigm is a solution for our epidemic of addiction and depression. Genetic predispositions aside, it's time to take responsibility for the insecure, fearful environment that manifests these debilitating problems. It doesn't take a rocket scientist to understand that addictions arise when there is no other effective way to comfort ourselves and relieve excessive stress. Addictions are an obsession with instant gratification to take away the pain and discomfort of living in constant fear. Depression is a different response to that fear—the chronic repression of negative emotions caused by a fearful, pessimistic view of the world and a fear of telling the truth. We have failed to stop the tide of depression with drugs. We have failed to eradicate addiction with slogans and clean needle programs.

We have failed to stop unethical behavior with more laws and more prison sentences, because control and punishment cannot replace the ethics that must be developed in each child by a new parenting paradigm that will help children develop a world-view that promotes integrity, self-esteem, personal dignity, responsibility, and a sense of connection to their spirituality and to their fellow man.

It's time to explore the link between living in a world that is overwhelmingly fearful and the deep despair that manifests as a result. We must all be willing to be accountable for the increasingly unsafe world perpetuated by this dysfunctional, debilitating paradigm that condones unethical behaviors in our families and communities. We must get busy educating ourselves and becoming truly mature adults. We must begin at once to practice radical integrity. We have the intelligence. The information is available. Being aware of our current paradigm can help you understand how dangerous and foolish it is to assume that you are a True Adult just because you are a grown-up or a parent. It can point you in the right direction to doing better. We all have things to learn and things to do, and the world needs you to do your part.

For too long we have looked for superficial fixes (such as control and punishment) to deal with deep and important ethical issues. As our prisons overflow, depression and addictions reach epidemic proportions, and suicide rates climb among increasingly younger children, we must be willing to look deeper for a solution. You can no longer afford to give somebody else or some institution the responsibility for the solution. You can no longer afford to let "them" handle it.

You are "them."

Understanding Children

"Reunite the joyful, imaginative child with the fully generative adult privileged to serve our precious earth."
—Jean Houston

Because we aren't born with a manual for being human or becoming an adult, we have to *learn* how to be an adult from a human model.

You came with a biological blueprint that unfolds, whether or not you got your real needs met. Of course, you also came with a unique genetic makeup, a set of unique personality traits and, in my opinion, a soul contract to fulfill. However, as a child, you were probably unaware of this. You were simply a bundle of motor, sensory, and emotional awareness that gradually got labeled by mental faculties, such as imagination, language, ideas, and beliefs. This mental labeling started long before your neo-cortex could make good decisions about what information was useful and what was damaging. If I had known the effect some of my early conditioning was going to have on my adult life, I certainly would have been a lot more discriminating about what I brought into it. My guess is that you would have done the same. But we didn't know; we were innocent and immature!

As John Bradshaw, one of our earliest experts on addiction says, "The main thing children want to know is that their parents are okay and that they *matter* to their parents." They know they matter when they get loving *attention*, physically, emotionally, and mentally. This is attachment. When that doesn't happen, when parents are unhappy, confused, unavailable, incompetent, or abusive, children take it very personally. Every neglected, abused child's inner cry is, "What's wrong with *me*?!"

When parents don't understand that children are by nature selfish and narcissistic, and that what children really need is attention, respect, affection, and genuine connection, it creates a deep wound. These are the things children require to develop into unselfish beings, aware of others as well as themselves. These things support the unfolding of our blueprint to its full potential.

Your deepest wound is the fear and shame that is caused by the belief that it's *your fault* your parents withheld what you needed because somehow, because of something unknown to you, *you didn't deserve it*. There's something wrong with *you*.

This wound holds pain in the deep unconscious part of your body/mind. It's also held in your energy field; Eckhart Tolle calls it the "pain body." The energy of the pain body continues to influence your life at an unconscious level, while you go through life failing to realize that you are attracting the very things that make you unhappy with this unconscious negative energy.

It's easy to feel like a victim when you have no idea that your own mind is attracting what you expect to you and that what you expect isn't very good! We all *want* good things, but if we don't expect them, or we have all kinds of pain stored in our body and energy field, they either don't show up or when they do, we will actually sabotage them. That pretty much describes the state of affairs on our planet today. We have a beautiful planet that is capable of providing abundantly for all of us, but we persist in believing in our unworthiness, whether consciously or not, and projecting that onto the planet and our fellow humans with profound disrespect. We don't believe there's enough for everyone because we don't experience ourselves as enough!

In our "mentally identified" culture, it's rare to encounter someone who is not terrified of the emotions and vulnerability that we were all born with. Young children haven't learned to squelch those emotions and they are, by their very nature, extremely vulnerable. Thus, they become deeply wounded in trying to accommodate to our society's expectations about showing emotions. They take the brunt of our cultural terror about emotional honesty. That doesn't alter the reality that William James expressed so well years ago: "One thing is clear: when we talk about human beings we can see that they are not driven by logic or reason. Ultimately, human beings are driven by their emotion—by their passional nature."

On top of that, we are obsessed with achievement and competition, as well as with control and punishment. Mired in fear and confusion about right and wrong, good and bad, and a myriad of dualistic beliefs that fail to take into account the paradoxical nature of reality, we allow children to grow up worshiping at the altar of the intellect yet lacking the critical thinking skills and the emotional awareness necessary for true intelligence. Intuition, a highly developed ability every child has, is treated with disdain and squelched. Grades are more important than knowledge. Telling teachers what they want to hear is more important than questioning assumptions and challenging ideas. I love these words by Anthony de Mello: "What is needed is not learning, but unlearning; not talent, but courage."

Because our current parenting practices, especially our disregard for and misunderstanding about the importance of attachment, do not do an adequate job of allowing us to move through the stages of childhood development without losing contact with our authentic self, our adult years are too often spent compensating for a sense of loss, unworthiness, and fear by using defenses that sabotage our life. We are so busy defending and protecting ourselves that our real thoughts and feelings get lost in all the confusion. We are too often unaware of what we *really* want or who we *really* are. If we do know, we're afraid to speak it honestly. There's no way you can function in a truly adult manner when you're so defended. As Margaret Paul would say, "We aren't open to learning when we are busy protecting." Protection always takes a priority; we're just wired that way. It's called "survival!"

The most damaging thing we do to children is force them to give up their own *inner* experience in order to be safe, accepted, and loved by their caretakers and others in authority.

Respect for others requires honoring what they see, how they feel, and what they want. If an adult knows this is in the best interests of the child, a choice that is more acceptable can be offered, without dishonoring the child, without punishing or shaming the child. It's so simple to say, "No, you can't have a hot fudge sundae because you had one yesterday (or there's no ice cream), but yes, you can have a cookie (or another treat) after you finish your dinner. Would you like this (cookie) or that (treat)?" Knowing how to make healthy choices is a critical skill that every child deserves to learn.

When you have lost contact with your inner experience, you have lost contact with the Divinity within you, the love that is your essential nature. How can you mature into a True Adult when you don't even know your true identity, how you feel, what you want, when you have accepted treatment that was actually abusive as "normal," when you have been betrayed by the very people you most needed to trust and actually been victimized as an innocent child? How can you mature into a True Adult when you don't know that many of the things you *think* you want are just substitutes for what you *really need*? Parents need to know what children really need and help them learn to distinguish between wants and needs. It doesn't take hitting and screaming to damage your self-esteem as a vulnerable child. All it takes is not knowing who you really are, how you really feel, what you really want and need, and not feeling comfortable about expressing all of that. All it takes is having your dignity and self-respect injured by having to give up your own authentic sense of self to earn your parents' attention and approval. Adults have incredible power over children. The abuse of this power breaks a sacred trust.

We are all born with a connection to the Divine, with an awareness of how things look and feel to us, and what we want and need. This awareness is our inner truth, which then becomes our identity when accepted and nurtured by our family.

Our authentic identity is necessary for the integrity that develops into an ethical system of values.

Creating an Adult

"People often say that this or that person has not yet found himself. But the self is not something that one finds. It is something that one creates."
—Thomas Szasz

Every child born deserves to live with True Adults who are willing to do these four things:

1. **Get educated about childhood developmental needs and commit to meeting them multi-dimensionally in ways that demonstrate respect for the dignity and sacredness of human life.**

Humility is a powerful thing. Learning is a lifelong endeavor. It is very humanizing and healing to admit there are some things you don't know and some things you need to learn in order to be a happier, healthier adult. Open up to both learning and unlearning; discover how exciting it is!

2. **Accept and nurture children's natural honesty rather than encouraging them to be deceptive and dishonest in order to avoid punishment.**

Be willing to hear the truth from your child. If it bothers you, there may be more truth than you are comfortable hearing, but it's an opportunity to grow. Listen anyway; become an expert listener, especially to children. Again, humility is powerful and your child will learn to respect your willingness to be open to learning. You can trust that you are modeling an important skill that will serve your child well.

3. **Be authentic with others, especially children, and allow others to do that with you.**

Reveal your authentic self to your children. This is a gift that will bear many fruits. It will ease the transition to adulthood for your children, giving them powerful permission to be authentic themselves. You are actually giving them your blessing to be who they are. It is especially important in adolescence, where authenticity can be an invaluable aid while transitioning to independence. Be willing to let go of relationships where you struggle with being authentic so your child will learn the same discrimination. As children mature, they become more aware of your faults. Knowing that they can respectfully challenge and question you will earn their trust. Be willing to learn from children. They have much to teach you.

4. **Create and maintain a True Adult to handle your own wounded Inner Child and to deal with the world in a mature, ethical manner.**

Whether or not you are upset with the ways your parents treated you, eventually you have to face the reality that you may still think and act much the way they did or you may be stuck in rebellion against it, which is far from being who *you* really are. That's what maturing calls for—questioning your beliefs and behaviors in the face of the negative results you are getting, then having the courage to choose better ones.

This was one of the more upsetting realities I had to face when I had my own children—I saw myself acting the same way my parents did, even though I had a long list of things I didn't like about my parents. I started questioning my sanity, my intelligence, and my character. In fact, that's what got me interested in studying psychology—I really wanted to do a better job than my parents had done and I finally had to face the fact that I didn't know how. First, I had to backtrack and reconnect with the God I felt abandoned by. I had to learn to trust myself. I had to learn to love myself. It's been quite a journey, with no guarantee that the results would be worth it. It's the hardest thing I ever did, but I can now say it's also the most rewarding!

Your Journey Starts Here

"What is possible—for the first time in human history—is an integration and fusion of the highest and most practical wisdom of all fields and disciplines to engender a new world and to work consciously and humbly with the divine to uplift the whole of humanity and the whole of nature into divine harmony, beauty, unity and power."
—Andrew Harvey

As a result of my own journey to adulthood, here's what I've learned about being a True Adult:

1. **A True Adult is willing to deal with reality, get educated, get help if necessary, and be fully accountable for the outcome of all situations.**

You are willing to take charge of getting informed and making choices that are in the highest and best good for all concerned. You choose learning over protecting your own false pride and false sense of self. You realize that this is the path to learning to love and embrace yourself, which is what self-esteem is all about.

2. A True Adult is self-authorizing and self-approving, willing to do what it takes to create a life that is personally rewarding and fulfilling.

You are willing to take risks and to nurture and explore your multidimensionality. You are willing to explore your emotional nature. You are willing to explore your passions and interests. You are willing to find solutions that reflect your true identity, cherished dreams, and personal goals, and to do this ethically and responsibly.

3. A True Adult has radical integrity.

You are willing to accept the consequences for all your choices, differentiating and discriminating between what is in your best interests and what is not, then choosing what is empowering for all. That is what personal power is all about: choice.

Choices that are good for you are good for others. By that, I mean that anything that is not in *your* best interests is really not in anyone else's best interests either. Sacrificing your welfare and happiness for others is not ultimately in anyone's best interests. A True Adult understands that only from that place of inner fullness is there plenty to share with others. Only a truly mature adult is capable of maintaining intimate, equal win/win relationships with others, flowing appropriately from dependence to independence as the situation requires. This is how mature interdependent relationships are created to acknowledge and accommodate both the need for closeness and for time alone.

Ultimately, True Adulthood requires taking back and giving up projecting your disowned self onto others. The main gift you can give to the world is to stop seeing *others* as the problem. You are not a victim! *Others are never your problem. Your own shame and self-hatred is your only problem.* You resent in others only that which you have disowned or misused in yourself. Your judgments about others' shortcomings are the key to discovering where *your own* denials and lack of awareness lie. Once they are discovered, you have the power of choice to do something about them.

Because they are committed to knowing themselves deeply and fully, True Adults are empowering to be around. They are secure in their own personal identity and disinterested in struggling with others. True Adults can be recognized by their willingness to treat others with respect and to forgive the past. Noticeable in their lives is a commitment to celebrating life's mystery and wonder on a daily basis by choosing love and trust and by expressing gratitude.

The *21 Ways* that follow are a model for a new paradigm. It provides a code of conduct that will enable you to become a truly mature adult, experiencing self-esteem, and capably and willingly empowering others because you are secure in your own power. You can then effectively impart ethics in your family and community. These *21 Ways* offer a practical, yet powerful model for radical integrity that you can use with everyone in your life, from bedroom to boardroom, to create the inner peace and outer harmony that can heal the world.

They are designed to assist you in your process of creating a truly empowered adult, one with radical integrity, who dares to feel, think, and behave in ways that may or may not agree with what you were taught or what others expect. Remember, the main goal is to awaken the compassion and wisdom that lies within you so that it will be natural and comfortable for you to act both powerfully and ethically. That is what empowers us to create a life filled with passion and adventure, the meaningful life we all deserve and the ethical life that is a gift to our children and to the planet.

"Never doubt that a small group of thoughtful, committed citizens can change the world. Indeed, it is the only thing that ever has."
—Margaret Mead

PART II

21 Ways

"What has been spoiled through man's fault can be made good again through man's work. It is not immutable fate that has caused the state of corruption, but rather the abuse of human freedom. Work toward improving conditions promises well, because it accords with the possibilities of the time. We must first know the causes of corruption before we can do away with them. Then we must see to it that the new way is safely entered upon, so that a relapse may be avoided. Decisiveness and energy must take the place of the inertia and indifference that have led to decay, in order that the ending may be followed by a new beginning."

"Since inner conditions are the theme of this hexagram, that is, work on what has been spoiled by the parents, love must prevail and extend over both the beginning and the end."

—*The I Ching*, Hexagram #18, Work on What Has Been Spoiled

Chapter 1

Personal Ways

"The superior man abides in his room. If his words are well spoken, he meets with assent at a distance of more than a thousand miles. How much more then from near by! If the superior man abides in his room and his words are not well spoken, he meets with contradiction at a distance of more than a thousand miles. How much more then from near by! Words go forth from one's own person and exert their influence on men. Deeds are born close at hand and become visible far away. Words and deeds are the hinge and bowspring of the superior man. As hinge and bowspring move, they bring honor or disgrace. Through words and deeds the superior man moves heaven and earth. Must one not, then, be cautious?"

—Confucius

Your first responsibility is to your own self. Unless you have small children who are totally dependent upon you or there's some emergency requiring that you put yourself aside for the moment, your job is to be aware of *you,* first and foremost. You must be aware of what condition your body is in, what you are perceiving, how you are feeling, and what you are thinking before you can come to another person with awareness. These things are your responsibility. Without awareness of self, it's too easy to get lost in other people's wants and needs and forget our own. It's too tempting to fall into the false role of taking care of others so they will owe you. Too many people are busy running the hidden agenda of expectation that their caretaking will earn them the love they desire. (And woe unto anyone who doesn't pay you back!)

Codependent relationships based on taking care of others rather than sharing from your own fullness are never fulfilling. Learning to be aware of all that's going on with you is a difficult task if you have been trained to take care of other people, worry about their well-being, and feel responsible for their happiness. These are some of the ignorant views that must be questioned and put aside. You can't make anybody happy who is committed to unhappiness. You don't help others by worrying about them; it is actually a sign of mistrust in their ability to handle life and doesn't help them at all. People can't respect themselves when they are forever depending upon others to do things for them that they are perfectly capable of doing for themselves.

Unfortunately, codependence is our paradigm for relationship. We are taught that it's selfish to think of ourselves first, but actually it's healthy. It is the only way to have fulfilling, equal relationships that are mutually satisfying. Interdependent relationships that start with self-awareness enable you to be clear about who you are, how you feel, and what you want. That is essential for maturity. Only then are you ready to engage with another in a mutually satisfying way.

1. Take responsibility for your self

You are multidimensional; it's up to you to take responsibility for all of you—your physical, perceptual, emotional, mental, and spiritual aspects. You are both yin and yang; you contain both masculine (dynamic) and feminine (receptive) energies.

Each of us possesses a self-regulatory, self-healing body (physical dimension), a multisensory capacity that is intuitive by nature (perceptual dimension), the full range of emotions or feelings (emotional dimension), a complex mental nature (mental dimension) with four different capacities (conscious, unconscious, subconscious, and super-conscious), and a spiritual dimension that is aware deep inside of its connection to the Divine. In addition, whether you live in a male or female body, you have a unique combination of both masculine and feminine energy (the capacity to both give and receive). Each of these dimensions and their various capacities require attention, nurturing, and maintenance.

The essential ingredient for optimal human functioning is balance. Any dimension that doesn't get its needs met disrupts the balance of your multidimensional system, leading to over-compensating in one capacity in an attempt to maintain balance in the overall system. Our secular society discourages the deep personal connection to our spiritual nature that makes life rich and meaningful. Our culture has also developed a sexist, homophobic, body-hating, and body-rejecting mentality out of distorted religious beliefs that the body should be scorned, punished, and relegated to a distasteful status. You are trained to ignore your intuition, deny your emotions, disregard or even damage your body, and identify mainly with your thoughts. This leaves you like a fine car, running on only a few cylinders when you have eight cylinders that can be used! This mental identification creates an imbalance that causes suffering and pain to humans.

Furthermore, there is widespread ignorance about the four capacities of the mental nature. You learn to identify with your conscious mind only and think this is reality. But you may fail to realize that your conscious mind is programmed by other people and may hold faulty, ignorant, even harmful information. Luckily, you don't need to be concerned about the subconscious mind, which takes care of your physical functioning below your awareness (thank goodness you don't have to think about breathing or any other bodily functions!). Learning how to tap into the superconscious, the part of the mind which connects us to our divinity, can be a comforting and worthwhile experience. The hardest part of your brain to work with is the unconscious. If you are ignorant about the contents of the unconscious, the part of your brain that stores painful experience until you are ready to deal with it, you are unaware of the things stored there that cause you suffering. Instead of learning how to tap into its wisdom, you learn to be ashamed of anything about yourself that fails to meet your family's or your culture's standards of right and wrong. All of us make mistakes because that's how we learn to be human. You were taught to deny and feel ashamed about the unconscious, repressed material that plagues you by creating your worst fears until you are willing to face your shadow and find the gifts buried there. This is important work that each of us must be willing to do if we are to heal our wounds and create inner peace.

You are energetically out of balance when you operate from only the energy of your gender, denying that its opposite lies dormant and ready to enrich your life. Any dimension that is not explored, developed, and nurtured robs you of the special wisdom provided by that aspect of your humanness, creating a distorted perspective of both self and world and limiting your capacity to deal effectively with life. The epidemic of depression we are witnessing today is caused by the chronic repression of the potent energy of the emotions coupled with a negative self-image and shame about our shortcomings. When you ignore your emotions and disregard or damage your body, you are eventually forced to put everything aside to heal the illness that inevitably occurs. Ignoring your intuition limits this important source of information necessary for guiding your life choices and developing the wisdom that is your birthright.

Reclaiming your multidimensional awareness liberates you from a restricted, confusing, depressing, unfulfilling personal agony. It invigorates the body, mind, and spirit, opening the heart to love and the mind to wisdom, and connecting you to your soul's destiny.

To Do:

1. Make a daily practice of exercise, a healthy diet, and adequate sleep.

2. Learn to recognize when you have emotions. Breathe into them and wait for inner guidance about what you want or need to do.

3. Get therapeutic help with your emotions and painful things you may have repressed (called "the shadow" or the dark side) if you are depressed. Your power is tied up here and you want to free it.

4. If you are male, get educated about your inner female; if you are female, get educated about your inner male. (See Way 4.)

5. Make meditation and quiet time a daily practice; it will awaken your intuition.

6. Reconnect with nature in any way that is enjoyable for you.

2. Refuse to be a victim

Master your fears—you are always at choice and it's your job to leave abusive situations or people, looking at your part in the conflict or problem.

Humans require the presence of certain behaviors in order to trust love. Those behaviors include respect, attention, approval, affection, and genuine caring. When those behaviors are absent, you instinctively do not trust that people love you, no matter what they say. Since your parents were imperfect humans, you have experienced to some degree the fear that comes from not trusting love. The absence of having basic physical and emotional needs met leaves a child feeling abandoned. Children are totally dependent upon the parents' giving these things in order to develop a sense of themselves as worthy and lovable. They are quite helpless to get it elsewhere for many years. To a young child, abandonment is tantamount to death. The child has no choice but to feel fear for his or her life.

Worry, pity, and caretaking often get substituted for genuine love, but in your heart you never really believe they are love. They are demeaning and disrespectful. They hinder the development of self-esteem. The absence of genuine love leaves in its place the most difficult human emotion—fear. When you have not been genuinely loved as a child, you grow up feeling afraid of life and of love itself.

If the withdrawal of "love" is occasional, these fears are an occasional annoyance leaving small scars. For some, whose parents leave altogether or whose presence includes abuse, neglect, or betrayal, the fear becomes all-consuming. Fearful people, young or old, don't feel powerful. The sense of powerlessness that is an inescapable part of such a childhood breeds a sense of one's self as victim—of others' whims, moods, and choices. Our parents are bigger, and smarter, and they are in charge. (If they're not, that presents a whole other set of problems, equally as devastating. Children are not ready to be parents or make adult decisions!) To the degree that you got your basic needs met, to the extent that you were given choices and responsibility and saw power used correctly, you either feel powerful or powerless. Too many of us have seldom seen power used correctly; what we mistakenly call power is actually the use of force to control people.

Our culture struggles with empowering children. We use control and punishment to impose our will on them. We tend to reinforce dependency and resist giving children independence in a gradual, empowering way. The result is grown-ups who still perceive themselves as powerless victims and who resort to victimizing others in order to feel powerful, just as they witnessed their parents doing to them. The misuse of power is a major problem on this planet, and each one of us can do his or her part to stop the victim consciousness that the chronic misuse of power perpetuates.

As an adult, you have a choice to refuse to remain a helpless victim. You can choose to be responsible for your own decisions and actions. It's empowering, both to ourselves and others, to refuse to be responsible for others, unless they are children or truly sick and incapacitated. Your task is to discriminate between the misplaced responsibility that enables others to be helpless victims and the sharing that comes from the overflow of your own abundance without needing or expecting anything in return.

To Do:

1. Make a list of all the people you feel responsible for, except for children and/or people who are paying you to take care of them.

2. List all the things you do for each person that these people are fully capable of doing for themselves.

3. Start with the person who would be easiest to speak to and tell him or her you want to renegotiate the relationship so the give-and-take is more even, more balanced.

4. Go through your list, one person at a time, until you have changed the way you relate to a more equal win/win status. Stop trying to fix them. Change your behavior and let go of anyone who insists on their right to be taken care of by you. This letting go may mean dropping this person or just pulling back your involvement to a more neutral place.

3. Embrace your Inner Child

Take responsibility for loving yourself by nurturing, accepting, and protecting yourself; heal your own wounds and let go of looking for somebody else to take care of you or fix you.

While your brain continues to develop throughout childhood and the teen years, your personal identity—your perception of who you are and how the world is—is pretty much in place by the age of seven. If your parents and family system provided you with the attention, affection, approval, respect, and caring necessary for experiencing yourself as valued and valuable and for seeing the world as safe, interesting, and wonderful, you were indeed lucky. Standing on this solid foundation, you can explore the world freely and create a great life.

Many (probably most) of us had less-than-perfect parents, operating from their own unresolved wounds, fears, and distortions about their own value, and you inherited any of the lacks and limitations they failed to face and make peace with. That's where addictions arise—they are your best attempt at numbing the pain you feel about not getting your real needs met by replacing them with addictive/compulsive behaviors. It's natural, even instinctual, for humans to try to find something or somebody else to fill whatever needs their parents failed to meet. That's what attracts you to friends, mates, and life situations—the hope that you will at last get what you need from somebody, or something.

The bad news is this means you will often attract people who aren't any more willing or capable of meeting those unmet needs than your parents were. On top of this, you may have also learned to feel "comfortable" (actually it's just familiar) with people who either can't or won't meet your real needs for safety, security, closeness, attention, and stimulation. Other unfulfilled people are all too often more than happy to engage in your addictions with you. In fact, often you're very uncomfortable with people who can and would meet your real needs! You are used to not being close and safe with people and are uncomfortable with people who could provide that closeness and safety.

The good news is you can heal this by being willing to face your own pain and discomfort. You can learn how to become your own parent, nurturing, protecting, and healing the part of you that carries your wounds as well as your potential for all things good. This Inner Child is who you really are, with your unique gifts and personality; it's the part of you that has access to your authentic self and to your Divine nature. Getting to know this part of you enables you to become an interdependent adult, capable of healthy, intimate, and fulfilling relationships with yourself and others.

To Do:

1. Adopt a doll or stuffed animal to represent your Inner Child so you can separate your developing adult from the part of you that is wounded and help it to heal. This separation helps you to separate from your wounds and become objective about the past rather than recreating it.

2. Talk with that doll every day and find out how it feels and what it wants, and be rigorous about taking care of those needs for yourself in healthy ways.

3. Provide daily nurturing and guidance for your Inner Child, but don't let it run the show.

4. Make sure your Inner Child is always safe and only comes out to play with safe people!

5. Get professional help if you were physically or sexually abused.*

*Note: Severe abuse is traumatic and requires good professional support for healing.

4. Access both masculine and feminine energies

You are made up of both masculine (dynamic) and feminine (receptive) energy. Experience and utilize both energies, rather than expecting the opposite sex to fulfill them for you.

The ancient Chinese wisely recognized that every living thing has both feminine and masculine energy. They called these energies *yin and yang,* and always pictured them together forming a whole. Masculine energy (yang) is dynamic, moving out into the world to accomplish things. Feminine energy (yin) is magnetic or receptive, attracting things from the outer world to meet its basic inner needs. Each energy is complementary to the other and necessary for living things to function.

Unfortunately, for centuries our culture has been in the throes of a patriarchal system that considers the female to be inferior, even though as fetuses we all start out female. Early on, humans are rewarded for stereotypic male or female behaviors and punished for those that don't fit the norm. We aren't encouraged to become whole people, utilizing both our masculine and feminine energies. When it's time to mate, you will often be unconsciously drawn to someone who you perceive will complete the traits of the opposite sex you have failed to develop. This can be both wonderful ("At last my other half is here!") and dangerous ("Now *you* can take care of things!"), depending upon the situation.

This codependent model of relationship is the standard for our culture; it is the paradigm we take on and it unconsciously determines our choice for a mate. Put simply, codependence leaves you wanting someone to love you even when you don't truly love yourself. Universal Law (the laws that govern energy) states that like energies attract other like energies. This means that when you don't love yourself, you will attract someone just like you. Each of you unconsciously expects the other to provide that which you don't have. To make matters worse, you then have trouble trusting that person's love and require constant reassurance. You are caught in a cycle of trying to earn that love but resenting your partner whenever he or she fails to love you the way you want (and not even realizing that your partner is doing the same thing to you!). The relationship becomes stuck in perpetual parenting of the other person, with both of you never quite succeeding at this impossible task. This parenting stuff makes it very hard for sexual attraction to survive! Some couples succeed by growing enough to recognize the changes they need to make. Others settle and put up with a sexless marriage; the ones who won't do this move on to the next relationship and keep trying to make this impossible formula work.

Ultimately, when you are dependent upon another for any magnetic or dynamic aspects you have neglected in yourself, you end up giving your power to that other in return for providing you with what you need. That feeling of powerlessness feeds your sense of being a victim and ends up inviting victimization. Maturing requires you to develop the ability to know what your personal needs are and take care of them independently. Each of us, no matter what our genitals, has the innate capacity to be responsible for functioning both magnetically and dynamically. Each of us can know what we need and then go out into the world to create it. This is true empowerment! This is the gateway to fulfilling interdependent relationships with others.

To Do:

1. Make a list of all the things you have trouble taking care of for yourself that are your legitimate responsibility, such as: feeding

yourself nutritious food; exercising to maintain fitness; getting adequate rest; and being responsible for your education, your friendships, your emotional balance, your spiritual well-being, and other personal choices that require your attention.

2. Prioritize that list, putting the things that affect your survival first, followed by your health, your emotional needs, your mental needs, and your social needs, in that order.

3. Make an action plan and enlist someone to hold you accountable for following it.

4. Do some reading and meditating about power: What is it? How does it feel? When do you feel powerful? When do you *not* feel powerful?

5. Get help with changing relationships where you feel you are struggling with power issues. If the relationships are abusive, you need professional help.

5. Honor your emotions

Learn how to feel and express your emotions in healthy ways; they give you important information about how you see your world and how it is affecting you.

Your emotions are the most accurate feedback you have about how the world is affecting you. They register as physical sensations designed to get your attention and tell you that things are either okay or they are not. Some say there are only two emotional states (with huge variations of intensity, of course): peaceful or afraid.

Many of us never learned to identify our emotions as children, so you don't need to feel guilty. This is an important part of emotional awareness. After you have learned what your feelings actually are called, then you can learn to deal with the more subtle nature of your emotions. Your emotions are caused by what you *perceive* is happening, which may or may not be what's really going on. That is why several people can witness the same event and have different stories and emotional reactions. When you both hear rumbling and the earth below is shaking, you're probably going to have a very instinctual reaction of fear. But you may run, while I freeze. That is because what you perceive and experience now is very dependent on early childhood experiences that are wired into your brain. Early memories and the emotions they evoked are re-created in the present time when similar situations occur. That's what makes it tricky to deal with emotions.

We humans have not done well with our emotional natures. Our culture is decidedly anti-emotion and it has failed to honor this valuable source of information. Too many of us learned to either repress emotions because they're just too uncomfortable or dump them on others, making them responsible for our feelings and manipulating or punishing them.

Many of us have learned to be afraid of things that are nothing to fear if faced. Yes, they are a figment of our conditioned minds, even though they seem like real threats! There are actually only two instinctual fears that all humans are born with: the fear of loud noises and the fear of falling. The rest are all learned. Some of them are real things to be afraid of, like earthquakes or fire, but most are not. They are projections onto the future by our conditioned mind, like expectations of disaster that we actually participate in creating because *we believe them and attract the energy to us!*

In order to be emotionally balanced and healthy, your task is to first identify that you're having emotions and then feel and release the energy that emotions create in some kind of *positive* action. Otherwise, you risk disease from the chronic storing of this dynamic energy, which eventually erupts somehow, somewhere, as a physical problem. You need to be willing to sit quietly with your feelings. You can learn to identify whether they are real or learned feelings. If something isn't happening right now in front of you, you may be dealing with your own perception, not reality. (You may be imagining someone doesn't like you when that's not true at all! It's really *you* who doesn't like you, but it seems like others who don't.) You can learn to allow the feelings to run their course, experiencing them as physical sensations, just breathing into them. As awareness of impulses to take action arise, you can make a wise decision (rather than an unconscious reaction) about what you need to do. (Maybe it's to ask the other person how they feel about you. You might learn a lot from asking this simple question.) Children can learn that skill as soon as they have words to describe their feelings, but it's never too late to learn how to identify emotions so their energy can be put to good use. They are a steady guide and trusted friend that can help you through life.

To Do:

1. Take time each day to sit quietly and breathe, allowing yourself to be aware of any physical sensations, thoughts, or feelings that arise.

2. Get clear about what you want or need; if you're not sure, discuss this with a trusted friend.

3. Take action on your wants or needs in a way that harms no one, especially not yourself.

4. When you have powerful emotions, release the energy physically by shaking if you're afraid, crying if you're sad, or shouting, pounding, or working out vigorously if you're angry. Discharge until the energy has subsided. Then go back to numbers 1, 2, and 3.

6. Welcome mistakes

You learn the most important things you know from making mistakes; so own them, correct them if you can, and learn from them.

Mistakes have a bad rep! If you looked honestly and closely, you would see that the most important and valuable things you know were learned by doing them wrong at least once or twice. You would also see that many things that upset you were never meant to hurt you; they're just someone else's truth. You have a choice not to take everything so personally. There's room in the world for *both* of you to be right, sometimes. Once you figure out what really happened, instead of what you *think* happened, you have a set of understandings and behaviors you can count on in the future without having to figure it out each time anew.

Sometimes you really are wrong. Now you have a choice: to feel guilty and upset; to fight a useless battle to prove that you are right; or to take the opportunity to learn something valuable. Remember that if you have never failed at something, you have been playing much too safe and too small. Fail proudly and know that you were out there trying and gaining information that will serve you somehow, somewhere you could never have imagined. It will, you can be sure. Every one of these *Ways* I learned from making many mistakes and finally choosing to learn something valuable from them.

Mistakes teach you the art of making choices. There is no skill more important. Life is about choice; at every moment you have a choice about how you perceive, how you act, how you feel, and how you think. Exercising the power to choose may bring a result that looks like a mistake. But if you look carefully, you will see that it's just a choice that got a result you have an opinion about. And it's your birthright to change your mind when you have better, or more, information. You are free to do as you choose about the results you get, and free to choose again and again.

In the end, there are no mistakes, only choices you must be willing to be accountable for. To be aware that you are free to choose and to be responsible for your choices is empowering. Your mistakes are trying to teach you something. They are trying to lead you somewhere that's very valuable for you.

Remember, you can choose to make lemonade out of your lemons. Tap into your creative genius—you were born with it!

To Do:

1. Write down the three most important choices you have made in your life.

2. Write down the results that you got from those choices.

3. Write down three positive outcomes from each of those choices (you may have to dig deep for these, but don't give up until you find them).

4. Write down the most important choice facing you today, and project both the positive and negatives outcomes you can imagine. Write about how the negative outcomes would affect you and whether you are willing to deal with those effects.

5. Make a choice and notice the results; if you are unhappy with the results, change your mind and do it differently.

7. Turn judgment into discrimination

Use your judgment to choose what to give your time and energy to and what to withdraw it from. This is judgment in its higher form: discrimination.

The mind judges; that's one of its jobs. These judgments help insure fulfillment of your primal need for safety and survival. The mind thinks in terms of good/bad and right/wrong. This helps assure your safety and survival. These polarities are also a reflection of the positive/negative, yin/yang energies that comprise the physical world. This ability is a necessary precursor for the mature thinking skills that enable you to discriminate between what is in your highest and best good and what is not. That's how wisdom develops. Mature adults learn to navigate the gray area of paradox that includes the yin and the yang of life, where everything is seen as a mixture of black and white, good and bad, right and wrong.

Too many of us never get to this paradoxical level of thinking. Seeing only the black or the white of things, many never mature into developing the ability to discriminate what is in their best interests. Are you stuck in good/bad, right/wrong judgments? You may require yourself and others to fit into one camp or the other, usually based on your early experiences and your parents' values, and then label the other camp wrong/bad. This is ultimately a very limited and limiting way to view life! It keeps you stuck in views that may not serve you at all.

If you had a painful, abusive childhood, you may often have low opinions about yourself that are very difficult to deal with. Nobody welcomes self-hatred; it feels shameful, and shame is a very painful emotion. Many of us are in denial about our childhoods and that we have shame and self-hatred. Many believe they are unlovable. Unhappy parents often project their own shameful, disliked traits onto their children, whether or not the children actually possess those traits. That's how projection happens: parents take the painful shame they don't want to feel about themselves, hide it in the unconscious, and then project it out onto others, especially their children. It actually looks to them like others are bad or wrong; then this is used as an excuse to reject, punish, or at least dislike and disapprove of others without examining themselves. That is judgment run amok and most of us learned to do this all too well. We are carrying painful loads of shame because of it, and it keeps us from loving ourselves!

The truth is, whatever you judge in others (with the accompanying shameful feelings) is a low opinion about yourself, either conscious or unconscious. These judgments reveal your own wounds. Your task is to reclaim these judgments by taking an honest look at them and doing some soul-searching about where these beliefs came from and what can be done about them to make them more healthy and useful. Mature adults have the right to choose how they see themselves and how they behave. Everybody wins when you stop looking down on others in order to feel good about yourself. These choices lead to healing and the development of true self-esteem, not to mention improved relationships with others. When we see ourselves with compassion, it's easier to see others in the same loving way.

Self-esteem is the prerequisite for self-love. It assists you in developing the art of compassionate discrimination, where you use your awareness to choose what kinds of situations and people serve your highest and best self and its interests. Then as you go through life loving and valuing yourself, you can share that overflow of love with others. You don't need to make others wrong in order to do what is right for you; there's plenty of room for all of us to do and have what we enjoy and let others do the same, even if it's not "our cup of tea."

To Do:

1. List all of the non-essential activities you currently engage in, such as watching TV, taking a nap, playing video games, chatting or texting on the phone, shopping at the mall. Rate each on a scale of 1 to 10 in terms of enjoyment and satisfaction.

2. Write about what you think would happen if you stopped doing everything that was less than a 5.

3. Either stop doing each thing or choose to continue because you are willing to do this activity for reasons other than enjoyment. Give up complaining about it.

4. Write a list of the people you currently feel judgment, dislike, or even hatred toward. Now write next to each one the ways you can see you are doing the same thing you accuse them of doing or holding the same traits. Ask a trusted friend to be honest with you about what he or she sees. If you don't trust anyone with this task, consider asking a professional therapist to help you with it. It can be very revealing and open the door to tremendous healing for you. Consider forgiving both the people you've listed and yourself for being human.

8. Ignite your passions

Take risks and explore what makes life exciting and meaningful to you, pursuing it with passion and commitment; support others, including children, in doing the same.

I am the only me in the universe, a unique expression of the Divine Creator. You are the only you in the universe, in all of the billions and trillions of Divine sparks that inhabit this infinite mystery we call life. Each of us has a unique personality, genetic makeup, and set of gifts and talents with their own challenges and rewards. Your ultimate task is to be aware of what grabs *your* interest, sustains *your* passionate involvement, and fulfills *your* heart and soul, mind and body. Nobody can make these assessments for you. You alone are responsible for following your bliss where it leads you. Only you can let go of what bores or stifles you, what hurts or damages you. I can't make you and you can't make me, as much as we may want to!

When you support others in following their own passions, it liberates you to follow yours. Taking the time each day to eat healthy foods, exercise, meditate, and spend time with yourself keeps you in fine tune, like a fine violin or guitar. All your strings are vibrating with a deep resonance that makes you feel good to be who you are and happy to be doing what you're doing. It helps release the toxins that you inevitably accumulate so you can hear that inner voice that speaks softly deep in the core of your being, calling you to what is right and best. Follow your own inner voice—it will never lead you astray.

As a culture, we especially need to encourage children to find their inner voice and listen to it. There is too much emphasis on controlling children and not enough on trusting them. Let them experiment with their passions; they all have them. Watch them, encourage them, but let them try things out on their own. If they make a mistake and need help, help without berating them so they grow up accepting mistakes as a natural part of life and the path to learning. This is their time to experiment and find out what makes life exciting for them.

Your time is precious. Wasting it on things that don't feed you in every dimension of your being will lead to regrets. Doing things out of obligation or duty will not fulfill you. Living out your parents' dreams may create nightmares for you. Your parents have no right to impose their dreams on you and you have no right to impose yours on your children. Their own destiny is calling them.

Your own destiny is calling you. Are you listening?! It is always the sweetest melody—your own!

To Do:

1. Give yourself an hour a day alone, either in nature or in a quiet place that is comforting and comfortable for you. You can sit quietly or walk or dance or meditate; try all of these things. Pay attention to your breath—it takes you inside. Focus on the navel area, which is the center of your body.

2. Use your time alone to let any thoughts, feelings, or desires arise in your awareness. Journal about them.

3. Make an action plan to address fears and manifest your desires. Then do it!

9. Learn your lessons

Accept everything and everyone as a gift that you have attracted to you for your own growth and healing; there are no accidents.

Just as there aren't any mistakes, there are also no accidents. Your life is perfect for you. Your parents, your childhood, your personal liabilities and assets—all these things are just right for you, no matter what the circumstances. Your soul chose this life because learning how to deal with all of this will make you more loving and compassionate, more wise and humble, more divinely aware and empowered.

Your energy acts like a magnet to attract the perfect people, situations, and events so you can exercise all your multidimensional capacities, learning how to make the best choices for your unique gifts and your destiny. Each person and event in your life has a gift for you if you are willing to look for it. Your task is to accept what you've attracted and use your skills to discern what you need to learn and what you can do better or differently.

Your next task is to be courageous, refusing to play the victim and blame others, especially your parents. This doesn't mean condoning others' bad decisions or behaviors; it means being willing to see why you have attracted them into your life, then stopping the judgment and moving into compassion so you can think clearly. It means refusing to let others stop you from pursuing your own dreams and desires. It means accepting that the goal of life is not to be happy; it is to become more aware of your true nature as a Divine spark of creation. Suffering is also optional. Give up the self-pity and get going toward a more fulfilling life.

You grow in stature, wisdom, and compassion when you welcome all that life brings—struggles, sadness, and even the pain of death, as well as joy, love, and the wonder of birth. It's all part of the great mystery of life that you are invited to dance. Truly embrace growing, changing, and evolving as the way that life unfolds. You are in the perfect place at the perfect time and all is in divine order. You can trust that.

To Do:

1. List all the so-called "accidents," disasters, and misfortunes of your life.

2. Look at each one and find the gift of courage, kindness, compassion, power, wisdom, and discernment that was a potential outcome of the event.

3. Be ruthlessly honest with yourself about whether or not you took the gift or squandered it. If you took it, honor yourself; if not, forgive yourself and then do whatever it takes to accept the gift.

4. If you have trouble with any part of this, seek counsel from a wise person who can gently guide you toward forgiving yourself so you can receive the gift.

Chapter 2

Interpersonal Ways

"Life leads the thoughtful man on a path of many windings.
Now the course is checked, now it runs straight again.
Here winged thoughts may pour freely forth in words,
There the heavy burden of knowledge must be shut away in silence.
But when two people are at one in their inmost hearts,
They shatter even the strength of iron or of bronze.
And when two people understand each other in their inmost hearts,
Their words are sweet and strong, like the fragrance of orchids."

—Confucius

Interpersonal relationships must be founded on equality. You are not exactly the same as any other human, but we are all equally human and we have the same needs. They just get expressed in our own unique ways. That's one of the crucial paradoxes about your humanity that you must accept: we are all the same, yet we are all different. It is in the understanding of this paradox that wisdom comes. We must all maintain both our separation *and* our unity—no small task!

Your special, unique contribution to all your relationships comes from your willingness to be authentic, to be the self that is real for you. To be authentic means to come from the place known as the core, located in the body, not the head. The head can be led astray, since the brain is both a transmitter and receiver of information. You can tune into others as easily as you can tune into yourself. Thus, your thoughts aren't necessarily your own. But when you can check in with your other faculties (or dimensions), you can come to know your personal truth. In the core of your body is a simultaneous awareness of what you're thinking, feeling, and wanting, all at the same time. This is *your* truth.

To be authentic means to come from that place of genuineness, realness, and truth when dealing with others. One who is authentic possesses integrity, which is a willingness to tell the truth as he or she sees it, of course with respect and kindness. In this way, you can have genuine, authentic relationships that are based on trust and truth. Thus, you can enjoy your unique separateness *and* your union with all others.

10. Be authentic

Honor who and what you genuinely and naturally are; speak the truth about it to others.

Wake up and get real! Belly up to your life. Be authentic and respect others' authenticity. Be present with yourself and then be present with others. Really show up and pay attention; then tell the truth, proclaiming to the world, "This is who I am; this is how I see it; this is how I feel; and this is what I want."

Be willing to do this in all of your dealings. Let others do this with you. Some people won't like it. If a place for you to be your real self can't be worked out with those others, you may decide not to play with them because you have chosen to be clear that you deserve to be with people who respect and enjoy who you uniquely and authentically are. You have chosen to believe that you deserve to associate with people who are in touch with their authentic selves enough to appreciate you for who you are.

You'll learn who you are most effectively through knowing others. That's because others are a mirror for you to look in and find out about yourself. What you like in others is what you embrace about yourself; what you dislike in others is what you've learned to deny or be ashamed of in yourself. So welcome all kinds of people and invite them to feel safe about being authentic with you by making it easy for them to tell you their truth, even if it's a complaint or criticism. Welcome diverse opinions and customs. Embrace diversity and celebrate life in all its rich possibilities.

Ah, it sounds so easy. It is, but you just can't imagine doing this if you have lost track of who you really are, how you really feel, and what you really want. Your task is to reclaim this by making your inner work the first priority in your life. You don't live in a vacuum, so you need to practice bouncing your authenticity off others. This is where you need support from others who are also committed to doing their inner work. Look for these people and watch the magic happen.

To Do:

1. Pick someone you trust and practice speaking the truth to that person on a regular basis. Let the person do the same with you. Use this simple formula: "I'm experiencing (how it looks to you); I'm feeling (mad, sad, scared, or hurt); I want (be brave and ask for what you really want)." Then ask if your friend is *willing* to give you what you want. Let the person say "no" without any punishment (see *Way 11*). Notice how it feels to do this and speak the truth about your feelings.

2. When you feel confident about your skills with your friend, try doing this with other friends. Notice how it feels to expand to a larger number of people.

3. If this is very difficult, find a support group led by a competent facilitator who can help you learn to communicate honestly and openly in a safe environment.

11. Maintain healthy personal boundaries

Say "no" to what you don't want; make it safe for others to say "no" to you.

Ever notice that all children say "no" before they learn to say "yes"? That's part of nature's plan to help us individuate from our parents, to separate from them and become our own autonomous selves.

Your personal boundaries are sacred, and no one should be allowed in your personal space without your permission and invitation. If your boundaries were disrespected as a child, you either failed to develop any personal boundaries at all and let people use and abuse you or you constructed steel-reinforced concrete walls that keep everyone out. Either way, you're in for a lot of pain because the kind of boundaries you have result in many relationship problems.

When you can't say "no" to someone, your "yes" is never fully honest. You are not in this world to be responsible for others unless it's a true emergency or unless and until you take on the responsibility of rearing or teaching children. You are here to take responsibility for your own care, nurturing, health, healing, well-being, happiness, fulfillment, and goals. You are here to share the abundance that you have created with others, not take responsibility for creating theirs for them. Even when you take on the responsibility for children, your task is to give them the opportunity and the tools to be responsible for themselves as they mature.

When you give this gift of respect to others, including children, you earn their love, trust, and respect. Taking care of others when it is their rightful responsibility to do it themselves is not loving; it's disempowering and insulting, and it robs them of the opportunity to experience true self-esteem. Healthy personal boundaries are one of the essential hallmarks of true self-esteem.

To Do:

1. Notice whenever you want to argue with people who disagree with you or say "no" to you, then keep quiet and let them speak.

Be honest with them about how hard it was for you to let them speak and thank them for being honest with you.

2. Make a list of the people whom you experience taking advantage of you. If there are none, congratulate yourself. If there are people on this list, how would it feel to tell them the truth and ask them to stop? If you are afraid to do this, seek professional help in facing your fears.

3. Make a list of the people you truly trust and to whom you feel close. If the only people on this list are your parents or mate and you know in your heart you are lonely and without close friends, seek professional help in facing the fears that cause you to keep people at a distance.

12. Claim your personal power

Never use your personal power to manipulate, control, or punish others; the only relationships that fulfill are equal win/win situations.

Power is a very difficult issue for humans. You want it because it makes you feel safe and secure. You don't want it because it's too much responsibility.

Many of us power struggle mightily with people in our lives. It ruins many an otherwise good relationship. You may have mistakenly seen power as *evil*. However, when power is misused it is actually more accurate to call it *force*, an imposing of your will, your energy, your might to make another do something you want. Control, manipulation, and punishment are a misuse of force that is damaging, harmful, and even evil. The results are inevitably painful and unfulfilling, creating mistrust and damaging relationships.

You may persist in using force against others in the mistaken notion that they have something you need or that you would be happier if they were different. Others can't make you happy—happiness must come from within. Those who use force against others are actually unhappy because they believe they are powerless and feel afraid. They don't understand what true power is and they don't know what to do to feel powerful.

The answer to the dilemma of power is to realize that it's unnecessary to take others' power because we all have power, whether we know it or not; it is inherent in our nature. Nor can you give others true power; what you are giving them is the right to hurt you, use you, dominate you, manipulate you, and torture you in a variety of ways. When you engage in power struggles with others, everybody loses because you have created an unequal, fear-based relationship.

That true power you seek comes from the Creator. The power that created the universe runs through you, always flowing freely from the source of power called love. This love is the energy that empowers and it is always available to you when you choose to connect to the source of power. By opening to receive that energy of love and then sharing it with others, you create relationships that truly fulfill because they are an expression of the truth that abundant love is ours for the asking. Will you receive? It is your birthright.

To Do:

1. Whom do you feel disempowered, weak, and afraid around? Write about what each one of those people has that you want and think you need.

2. Make a plan to find what these people have inside *yourself,* and begin to use it every chance you get. Get professional help if this is difficult.

3. Make a list of everyone you have ever punished (including children) and apologize for your behavior, resolving to stop this kind of behavior, and giving these people permission to tell you whenever they experience you trying to punish, control, or manipulate them.

4. Commit to a daily spiritual practice so that you maintain a constant connection to the source of power and love.

13. Let go of blame, punishment, and control

Take responsibility for your negativity, judgments, and feelings—they are actually about you.

Our opinions and feelings about others are tricky. It is important that you start to question why you are having those opinions and the feelings they stir up. They have far more to do with you than with the other person involved. You want to get interested in that!

The mind is made to judge. It is always taking in information and making decisions about what to do with that information. Much of the information you have in your mind is connected with emotions, positive and negative. When you have negative emotions and beliefs about yourself, you tend to do one of two things with that information: feel inadequate, ashamed, and unworthy, or deny you feel bad and repress the feelings because they're painful.

When you repress these negative feelings and thoughts, they pop up everywhere through the mechanism called *projection*: seeing others through your own filters, be they positive or negative. What you see out there is what you *expect* to see. Another way of describing this is that your mind is like a video, projecting what you perceive (based on early experiences imprinted in the midbrain) out onto the world and calling that perception "reality." Sometimes you will find outer things that fit your projection well; sometimes you are in total delusion about what you think you see in others.

If you want to have fulfilling relationships, the first step is accepting that this is what's going on between people. If you see things you don't like in people, whether it's real or imagined, you will find it time-and-energy-consuming to try to change others so you are more comfortable with them. When you accept that the reason you're uncomfortable has more to do with *you* than with them, you now have an opportunity when you see something in yourself (through looking at them) that you don't like. You are in an empowered position to make changes in yourself, in your own thoughts and behaviors. Try it. It's amazing how this solves most relationship issues. Others seem to change before your very eyes when *you* change.

To Do:

1. Make a list of all the things that bother you about other people.

2. Ask at least five people to give you honest feedback about how they see these things in you. Be sure to make it safe for them to tell you the truth. Just listen and don't defend yourself; then thank them.

3. Write down each item and spend some time getting clear about what fear causes you to act this way. If you have trouble with this, get professional help.

4. After you have finished with an item so you feel clearer about it, practice a more empowering behavior for one month or until you feel you have mastered it. Go on to the next item and repeat until done; get feedback regularly.

14. Keep your commitments

Have the courage to do what you say you will do or renegotiate if you change your mind.

I love this simple formula for getting good results in life: walk your talk. I've heard it attributed to American Indians, but regardless of their background, people on this planet don't always do so well at doing what they say they will do. I believe you're always doing what you're *really* committed to even though you're not conscious of it; you're just not telling the truth about it, to yourself or to others, often because you're unaware of it. Your motivations are unconscious because you've learned that they're wrong or disgusting or some other negative thing. So you hide your motivation and act unconsciously!

If you want fulfilling relationships, they must be founded on trust and respect. If you say something, you need to mean it. If you say you'll do something, you need to do it. If you change your mind and don't want to do something or can't, you also need to be honest about it. You can't expect others to trust or respect you when you don't tell the truth, when you don't do what you say you're going to do. Others notice this; if they don't, it's because they don't *want* to notice. Maybe they would rather believe their own fantasies about you than know the real you.

It takes a lot of courage to tell people the truth and then act on it, especially in the face of others' disapproval, judgment, or anger about it. But not telling the truth just creates self-judgment and low self-esteem, so you must be willing to accept the consequences of duplicity. You are not responsible for others' opinions of you. No matter what you do, some will approve and some won't. The person you look at in the mirror is the main one you're responsible for and you have to live with that person. Telling the truth about important matters is the only way to feel good about your reflection.

The person you are is not set in stone; it is always growing and changing. What suits you today may not tomorrow. We all benefit from being flexible with our choices, aware that what looks good today may not look so inviting tomorrow. We all have the right to change our minds. Don't let anyone take that away from you. Just communicate the change as soon as possible so that others can make adjustments.

To Do:

1. Make a list of the promises you know you've broken and feel guilty about. Ask all the people close to you (both personal and professional) to give you a list of the things they are disappointed about or hurt about that you have done.

2. Apologize, then either take care of the broken commitments or renegotiate until everyone is satisfied. If this is difficult, seek help from a third person who can negotiate a win/win for both parties.

3. Make a list of any things you have committed to doing that you really don't want to do. Be honest and renegotiate the commitment by going to each person and telling the truth about your desire to renegotiate with him or her.

4. When you make a commitment, write it down and then cross if off when it's fulfilled.

5. Be rigorous about communicating anytime you change your mind.

15. Give without agendas

Learn the difference between sharing from abundance and caretaking; stop robbing yourself and others of the opportunity to achieve self-esteem and dignity, and give up doing things for others they should and could do for themselves.

There is a learning model that depicts a four-stage process of growth for humans. The first stage is called "unconsciously incompetent," or what has been described as "not knowing we don't know." Put simply, we are not aware that we don't know certain things when we start the learning process.

What has this got to do with agendas? All humans need things from other humans—we are born very dependent. Gradually you become more independent and learn how to meet your physical needs. Some of your needs, such as affection, attention, respect, caring, and appreciation, legitimately require others to fulfill throughout your life. The self-nurturing activities that keep your body healthy, your heart happy, and your mind alert are best done by your *own self.* Those acts of self-love raise your self-esteem, your sense of dignity and worth, and provide you with the inner experience of competence that is so necessary to functioning effectively in the world.

If you got your dependency needs met as a child and had parents who then encouraged you to become independent and learn the skills of self-care, you know what to do and you do it. If you didn't get those needs met, you may not be consciously aware that you still want things from people. You may have a huge vacuum to fill and will instinctively try to find someone to do that, even if you're fully grown. You will unconsciously be attracted to others like you who are willing to play out the caretaking role to fulfill that inner emptiness. It becomes a trade-off game: "I'll do this for you, if you do that for me." In some relationships that may *seem* to work to create a balanced give-and-take. Problems occur when one person decides to stop the game and the other one doesn't want to stop. The balance is disturbed. The two halves that made a whole unit cannot function when one person decides to become a whole, independent person.

A truly fulfilling relationship is synergistic: two whole people creating much more than the sum of two. When you spend your life taking care of the needs of others that are legitimately *their* responsibility, you enable them to remain powerless, helpless, and dependent upon you. You may end up incurring resentment for all the time and energy the other took from your own passions and goals. Everyone suffers where resentment resides.

Let go of controlling others with your giving. Just open your heart and give freely. You'll find that it always comes back in the most perfect way at the most perfect time.

To Do:

1. Make a list of all the things you resent that you are doing for others. If you find that you resent many if not most of the things you do, especially for your children, consider talking to someone you trust or get professional help with understanding the source of those resentments.

2. Stop doing them. (This includes what you do for children, after they have started school.) If someone on your list is incapacitated, find someone else to do the thing you resent and pay that person if necessary.

3. Give others permission to stop doing things for you that they resent. These acts are really hidden agendas, and you must tell people you are aware of their agendas. You must give up wanting

others to do things for you out of a sense of duty (probably so you feel loved). Take them off the hook! Let them express their love in ways that they want to.

4. Be rigorous about taking care of your personal needs and responsibilities so you have a full cup from which to give.

16. Celebrate your sexuality

Honor and take care of your body; meet your sexual needs, either with a consenting adult partner or by freely chosen celibacy.

A look at the average body in our culture would shock a visitor from another planet. We starve it. We stuff it. We resent having to take care of it. We resent that it doesn't fit some idealized picture of perfection. We resent its needs, its feelings, its ever-present demands for attention, care, and nurturing. Too many of us just don't like having bodies. And it shows!

Many of us believe bodies and their functions are dirty and disgusting. More than anything else that the body does, many of us think sex is the most dirty and disgusting thing of all. Some of us shut down all awareness of our sexuality and think it's irrelevant; we are unconscious about it and deny having any feelings at all, sexual or otherwise. Others of us obsess over it. Either way, sex is something that must be reckoned with. To ignore its powerful energy is to risk having serious health problems and frustrating sex lives.

We are not allowed to explore our sexuality without feeling ashamed, without sneaking or flaunting it. We either resort to repressing our sexual needs or we use sex as an addiction to comfort ourselves when we're in pain. We are inundated with sex, using it as a commodity to sell our products and ourselves, yet how many of us are truly sexually fulfilled? Many women fake orgasm or have given up the hope of having one. Many men have never experienced a full orgasm, content to just ejaculate. Masturbation is still controversial—talked about but often done only with guilt.

Parents are embarrassed to talk about sex with their children. Schools still argue about whether it's an appropriate topic and then offer watered-down anatomy lessons, avoiding the deeper issues of sexual intimacy, lovemaking, and contraception. We are a homophobic society, still arguing about whether certain kinds of sex are sinful and secretly believing it's all sinful, truth be said. Homosexuality, bisexuality, and transsexuality are still topics that defy acceptance and bring up shame.

What a mess we're in! Imprisoned in bodies we reject, we look for ways to escape. We are anything but sexually liberated. We don't have permission to explore all aspects of sexuality or even to freely choose celibacy: instead it's imposed by the rules of religion. The sexual revolution has not arrived yet—we've merely swung from one extreme (a religion-imposed repression of our sexual needs and desires) to the other (a full-on hedonistic addiction to the darker aspects of sex and pornography). Until we learn to love our bodies and to harness the power of our sexual energy in the service of the best and most beautiful aspects of human nature, we will not be at peace as a species.

Sexuality is a source of tremendous energy and power. Repressing it doesn't work; it just goes underground and wreaks havoc. In humans, it's elevated by the love that it expresses in a totality of fusion that only sex provides. An orgasm is known as "a little death" in French, because it contains so much power that one is transported to another realm for a brief time. A shared orgasm delivers the ultimate in ecstasy. That much power and energy cannot and should not be ignored. Do yourself a favor: embrace your sexuality and explore its potential for radiant health and well-being!

To Do:

1. Start waking up your body. If you don't exercise, start now, anywhere. A walk around the block will do, in the beginning. Increase it as you get used to it. If you compulsively exercise, take a day off once or twice a week and enjoy a bubble bath instead.

2. If you don't masturbate, learn how to do it lovingly; if you masturbate compulsively, take a week off and journal about the frustrations, fears, and pains around your sexuality. What feelings are you covering up with your addiction to masturbation? Be willing to be honest with yourself. Share these feelings honestly with someone you trust.

3. Stand naked in front of the mirror and make an honest assessment of what you like and don't like about your body. Make an action plan to take care of the things that you can change. Commit to learning how to accept the things that can't be changed. Your attitude about your body is important!

4. Learn to meditate, sitting quietly for at least fifteen minutes a day, focusing on your belly and breathing deeply. Be present in your body. Journal about your experience.

5. Get a makeover at a department store and consider changing your wardrobe to more adequately show off your body's best features. Stop hiding yourself in your clothes. Get professional help if you feel overwhelmed.

17. Cultivate Intimacy

Have the courage, humility, and vulnerability to face your fears of being known and seen by others, and share yourself freely with those who have earned your trust.

Most of us are afraid of intimacy, whether we would admit it or not. We want it, but it scares us to death. Why? Because our parents or caretakers—the people we most wanted to be close to—hurt us when we were young and innocent and vulnerable. We opened up in an honest, vulnerable way and they responded with something that hurt us. If they were uncomfortable in their bodies, afraid of their sexual power, and terrified of their emotions, they held us at a distance and taught us to do the same. They had no idea how to heal their own childhood wounds—that concept didn't even exist for them. Uncomfortable with letting us get really close, close enough to deeply experience them, warts and all, they passed their discomfort on to us. And we closed down to them to protect ourselves.

You need intimacy, just as you need air and water and food. You need to feel safe enough with at least a few people to touch them, let them touch you, and speak the truth about how you see things and how you feel. You need to trust that, no matter what, they won't reject you.

That's intimacy—knowing and being known, deeply and fully. Other than our physical survival, nothing matters more to humans. And because we were hurt as children, betrayed in our need for a deep, intimate connection with our parents, we suffer from alienation and loneliness more than any other species. We call this "failure to attach."

Attachment is a basic need we all were born with. Every child learns how to be human by attaching to its parents. This attachment involves a deep and authentic sharing between mother and father with the child at every level, physical, perceptual, emotional, and mental. It requires sharing thoughts and feelings, touching and being touched in an authentic way. It requires time and energy on the parents' part but in today's busy world, that time too often is neglected. Children spend more time with babysitters than with their parents. Children fail to thrive because their parents are busy, preoccupied, angry, hurt, and a wide variety of things that have nothing to do with the child, but that the child takes very personally. So to protect itself, the child shuts down and puts on a phony face and a good act. Or the child becomes angry and rebellious, not necessarily understanding why.

It takes tremendous courage to feel those fears of being known and open your wounded heart to others. It is an act of profound bravery to be vulnerable, tender, and genuine. It's the only way out of your pain. You can do it. You must do it. We will destroy our species if we continue to forget that others need us as much as we need them. We're in this together.

To Do:

1. Make a list of all the people you feel betrayed by, unloved by, hurt by, et cetera. Write a letter to them and pour out your heart. Ask for what you need from them to help you heal this wound. Notice the similarities between your parents' behavior towards you and the type of wounds that others have inflicted. Get professional help if the emotions become too intense.

2. Send the letters that you can send; read to someone safe the ones you can't send.

3. Grieve. Feel the pain and release it. Take as long as you need for this process. Again, it may require professional help to go through this process.

4. Join a safe support group where people share openly and heal their fears about intimacy.

Chapter 3

Transpersonal Ways

"To bless means to help. Heaven helps the man who is devoted; men help the man who is true. He who walks in truth and is devoted in his thinking, and furthermore reveres the worthy, is blessed by heaven. He has good fortune, and there is nothing that would not further."

—Confucius

The transpersonal is about the ultimate relationship you have—the one with the Creator, the Divine, the relationship that makes you abundantly aware of your connection to All That Is, to the whole universe. The transpersonal realm is where you connect to other living things, in fact, to *all* living things. The transpersonal allows us to practice what is known in Africa as Ubuntu: I need you to be me and you need me to be you.

This realm also connects you to your purpose in life, the one you took on before you were born. It gives your life a sense of meaning and purpose as you go through the many facets of life. It provides you with a beacon in the dark as you search for what feels right to you and for you. We are all born with that sense of connection. We intuitively search for that meaning as children, but because our brains are not fully developed for the first twenty years of life, our understanding is often confused. On top of that, our minds are conditioned by our parents and culture to accept many things that are not true and many things that are actually quite destructive to living life with a sense of our worth and dignity. And so we lose awareness of our Divinity, of our wholeness and perfection.

Much of what makes life difficult yet worthwhile comes from the search for connection to who you truly are, that seeking for wholeness and perfection. As you mature, you more and more clearly see the perfection in your imperfection and begin to understand what paradox is. And paradox is ultimately where you find truth.

It's been said that we create God in our own brains, the part of the brain that wonders why we are living and what the meaning of life is for us. This search is your ultimate task and your ultimate goal. Thus, questions, not answers, are the stuff of life. Enjoy the search for meaning! Don't settle for anyone else's meaning—find your own. It will just feel right when you find it.

18. Surrender to your Higher Self

Develop and utilize your own spiritual nature to access the love, wisdom, and power that are available to every human.

Of course, you want to trust that things will work out for you, but sometimes it really doesn't look as if they will. If you remember that airplanes don't fly straight, they actually zigzag to their destination, you can do the same—flow with life's twists and turns. You will take what look like wrong turns and make what look like serious mistakes. No human can avoid this. The best way to get through life is to accept this and be willing to turn to the still, small voice inside that is connected to the truth about who you are and why you're here.

We all have that voice, but we live in a culture that doesn't promote finding or listening to it. Instead, we are trained to accept outer authority. However, there are many techniques and tools readily available to help you learn to find the authentic self that lies within. It's imperative that you choose to do so or life's storms and uncertainties will overwhelm you. Sometimes those storms overwhelm you anyway, despite your determination to trust your process, to listen to the inner voice and to follow your own drumbeat.

There are two things that will carry you through the difficult times: the inner work of meditation and the outer support of others on this path. The inner work involves going inside and connecting to the Source of wisdom, love, and power that is always there, waiting for you to ask for guidance. Reaching out for the support and assistance of others on this path reminds you that you are not alone in the world. You are part of a beautiful tapestry of many shapes, sizes, and colors that creates a glorious Whole that is called Universe or God or whatever holy name has been devised to speak of the mystery that is beyond words.

There is no higher commitment you can make than to staying true to your Higher Self as you journey through life. It is really the only security any of us can count on. Things, people, life situations—they all come and go. The eternal Now lives within you and links you to the mysterious, awesome power of eternity.

To Do:

1. Commit to a daily meditation practice and incorporate it into the routine of your life, just as you would do with exercise, diet, sleep, and other basic care.

2. If meditating is difficult, find a teacher who can guide you.

3. Explore groups that meditate together and find one that feels safe, empowering, and supportive, one that doesn't force you to buy into some dogma or rigid set of practices that usurps your own inner authority.

4. Read inspirational material and glean the wisdom of others who have explored the spiritual path.

19. Trust the process

Surrender to your built-in healing process, trusting that it will lead you to the inner wisdom and the unique gifts that will create the perfect life for you, including right work and right relationship.

Quit trying to figure out how to fix yourself. The only real problem you have is that you *think* there's something wrong with you, or that you think you *are* a problem. The truth is you are just a person with your own personality, gifts, and lessons, just like the rest of us.

No matter what disguise it assumes, every person on this planet is here to learn about love. It must start within you. In order to really love yourself, you need to trust yourself. In order to trust yourself, you need to be connected to the small inner voice that knows and speaks the truth (while your brain may be yapping away about nonsense).

As you do the inner work of letting go of limiting and false beliefs, you're left with some important choices. These choices are always optional and only you can make them. One is to forgive yourself for believing there was ever anything to fix; the other is to learn to go within so you can have your own awareness of the inner experience that creates trust and love. You can access this inner knowing when you're willing to be quiet and still. In the stillness, you can access the Source energies that power your own built-in healing process in a most mysterious and wondrous way. You may never fully figure out this process but you must be willing to let it happen, instead of fighting, resisting, and trying to control it.

Your willingness to do whatever it takes to hear that small inner voice is your work; Source does the rest. Eventually that voice grows louder and stronger. Your inner voice is the voice of God within, showing you the way; it never fails you even though you may not always like what it says. Your surrender to this voice ultimately leads you home, where you are always safe, loved, and whole. It leaves you empowered to be a force for love, light, and goodness in the world.

To Do:

1. Your responsibility is to maintain healthy personal habits, physically, emotionally, and mentally. If you're not sure what is healthy, read books, go to classes and seminars, get a therapist, or join a support group.

2. If you're still practicing addictions and numbing out with them, get help with those first, because they will impede the healing process by keeping you emotionally numb, mentally confused, and physically toxic. There are free programs like Alcoholics Anonymous and its many offshoots that can help with this. Get past your denial that you're in the grips of addiction and seek help!

3. Hang out with people who are also doing their healing work and avoid people who are not—they may be uncomfortable with what you're doing and try to manipulate you into staying addicted so they don't have to feel their own pain.

4. Did I mention meditation? I think you get it. Now do it! This will provide you with help from Source, God, or whatever other name you call it. The comfort is real, and it helps you stay more and more calm and centered. Just keep doing it!

20. Love unconditionally

Love, appreciate, acknowledge, and approve of yourself rather than seeking those things from others; forgive yourself for all your shortcomings and mistakes, make amends if necessary, and then commit to being kind, compassionate, and loving to others, whether it is reciprocated or not.

Give what you want to get. Then stop resenting the people you give to for not giving back the way you wanted. If you pay attention, you will see that your giving always comes back to you somehow, somewhere, just not necessarily as you expected. But it will be perfect!

Giving up expectations and assumptions about what your actions will cause is an important part of your healing. Most of your assumptions are unconscious beliefs that you would benefit greatly from challenging and amending. They come from the Inner Child part of you that is afraid you're not worthy of life's goodies and always wanting others to prove to you that you're really good enough. You have to give that up; it keeps you stuck in the past and coming from a place of inferiority that doesn't serve you in any positive way.

Let others be and do what they want. If you don't like it, you are always at choice to leave, to move away from the person and/or situation. Move away from what causes unhappiness, frustration, and pain; move toward what creates happiness, fulfillment, and well-being. Others are only doing the best they know how to do and it's not your job to change them or fix them. It's your job to stop participating in their pain and to start creating your own happiness. If and when they're ready to change, they'll notice you are doing things that work and they may ask you about them. Meanwhile, commit to the full-time job of keeping your own life on track.

Nurturing, protecting, healing, and empowering yourself take a big commitment. Doing that is how you love yourself unconditionally. Every moment is a moment of choice. Do the best you can right now and let go of punishing yourself for mistakes from the past. The past is gone; you are at choice NOW! Choose love and trust; let go of doubt and fear by facing them and making a choice that works for your highest and best good. You deserve it. You always did.

To Do:

1. Give up your control dramas, the ways you control and manipulate others so you don't have to feel the pain of your own wounds. That means no more bullying, no more whining, no more caretaking, no more seducing, no more withholding, no more "nice guy" or phony Pollyanna stuff, no more helpless victim. No more.

2. Enlist your friends in calling you on your control dramas and make it easy for them to be straight with you about how they experience you. If it hurts, they're right on the money. Thank them, and change the way you think and behave.

3. When you're upset with others, be fully accountable for how that exists in you and use it to change your ways. Give up trying to change them. Leave if it's really unsafe to stay, but notice you were there for a reason and learn the lesson.

4. Give what you want to get. Let go of expectations about the results.

21. Make peace with paradox

Learn to hang out with paradox, which is where the wisdom, love, and power of the universe are available for your creative pleasure and fulfillment.

The highest order of thinking is paradox, that nebulous place where everything is one, where the opposites come together in unity, where what is right can also be wrong, and vice versa; where black and white become gray and yin and yang meet and merge in a cosmic dance of creation.

The brain is physically structured in two hemispheres, with a corpus callosum that allows the two lobes to communicate. This is not fully developed in the brain until about age five, so you're incapable of higher thinking as a young child. The brain increases in size at the end of the teen years so you can move into adulthood with a structure that can share information from two opposing sides and create the best possible choices in life.

Likewise, in the physical world, things exist in opposites. Male and female seem different; opposites are the way most things are arranged. Everything in the physical world actually starts out female and only becomes male if a certain genetic message is given. In other words, masculinity is inherent in everything feminine, no matter how it develops at the physical level.

But in the unseen world, these opposites occur very differently. At the microscopic level, waves of energy and particles of matter appear and disappear in infinite patterns that are seemingly chaotic, yet always arrange to interact in some form that joins the eternal web of creation. These waves and particles actually respond to thought, so never forget how powerful your thoughts are.

While the physical organ we call the brain may struggle with all of this, the mind that registers your conscious awareness can live in this paradoxical world quite nicely. The brain actually works by asking questions like "why" and "how." It wants answers because it's got a job to do. Yet the mind rejoices in mystery, awe, and wonder. Each mind is capable of merging with the cosmic Allness that we call Universe or God, where you can experience the seen and unseen potential of which we are all a part. Your mind lives in and through the physical body. Nurturing the body nurtures the mind that can tap into the love, wisdom, and power that make human life a precious mystery and an awesome gift.

To Do:

1. You are not your body, but you live in one. Nurture your body. Dance, play, make love with yourself and your beloved.

2. You are not your emotions, but they are powerful messages that you must feel and express in ways that do no harm to yourself or others. Take up an art form to express your emotions—write, paint, make music, dance, cook—anything can be art.

3. The conditioned mind is a mental program that runs automatically in your midbrain; you are not those beliefs and you can and must dis-identify with them by disregarding those that don't serve you. You are liberated by choosing what it serves you to believe and what you need to disregard. Your mind is designed to be your servant, not your master. Master your mind.

4. Learn to meditate on a regular basis. This daily practice connects you with the infinite, with the part of you that is connected to and one with the Universe. It makes you aware of being more than human, more than your problems and concerns. It makes you feel at home with yourself and at one with the all that surrounds you. It helps you to pay attention to your own experience and learn to honor it. It brings great comfort to know that you are one with that Allness we call God.

Bibliography

The following is a partial list of books that have contributed to my thinking:

John Bradshaw, *Homecoming (Reclaiming and Championing Your Inner Child)*
John Bradshaw, *Healing The Shame That Binds You*
Nathaniel Branden, *The Six Pillars Of Self-Esteem*
Jean Illsley Clarke & Connie Dawson, *Growing Up Again*
Robert Firestone, *The Fantasy Bond*
Debbie Ford, *The Secret Of The Shadow*
R. Buckminster Fuller, *Critical Path*
Shakti Gawain, *The Four Levels Of Healing*
Harville Hendrix, *Getting The Love You Want*
Harville Hendrix & Helen Hunt, *Giving The Love That Heals*
Harville Hendrix, *Keeping The Love You Find*
Harriet G. Lerner, *The Dance Of Anger*
Harriet G. Lerner, *The Dance Of Connection*
Harriet G. Lerner, *The Dance Of Intimacy*
Michael Lewis, *Shame: The Exposed Self*
Thomas Lewis, Fari Amini & Richard Lannon: *A General Theory Of Love*
Margaret Paul, *Inner Bonding*
Margaret Paul, *Healing Your Aloneness*
Joseph Chilton Pearce, *Evolution's End*
David Richo, *Shadow Dance*
Sandra Riggins, *Breaking The Cycle*
Gabrielle Roth, *Maps To Ecstasy*
Eckhart Tolle, *The Power Of Now*
Alberto Villoldo, *Illumination*
Charles L. Whitfield, M.D., *Healing The Child Within*
Gary Zukav, *The Dancing Wu-Li Masters*
Gary Zukav, *The Heart Of The Soul*
Gary Zukav, *The Mind Of The Soul*
Gary Zukav, *The Seat Of The Soul*

33639505R00069

Made in the USA
Lexington, KY
03 July 2014